Instant *Idiot*

Just Add Alcohol

Sonny Carbo

PAGE PUBLISHING, INC.
New York, NY

First originally published by Page Publishing 2014

ISBN 978-1-62838-474-1 (pbk)
ISBN 978-1-62838-475-8 (digital)

Printed in the United States of America

Acknowledgments

The author would like to thank the many people that have helped in one way or another over the years.

There is a mother that never gave up and sisters that were there when nobody else was. There was a brother that did all he could and great brothers in law. The love of my life for 23 years. She taught me so much; I will always miss her. There was medical staff that did all they could to restore my health knowing I'd be back, and the 12 step group they sent me to that saved my life. Thank you for the miracle of recovery. A sister in law I've been friends with a long time, and another long time buddy. Two great ladies that helped me put this book together. Their expertise in the critique, format, printing, etc. was in-valuable.(To all the places of employment that I cheated or stole from.)

I am grateful to have been born in the United States where I was given more than one second chance, my church that invited me into the church family, and to God, who without I am nothing.

Contents

A Friend...7

Evolution 9

How Could this Happen...11

Off to a Bad Start 14

Off to a Good Start 17

Depression..20

A Will to Survive 22

The Monster 24

Only by Faith can Inspiration Come from Inadequacy 25

Get Some Help..28

About Alcoholism and Depression 30

Moral Defect 39

Long Recovery Period..41

Another Attempt 44

Suicidal...46

Addictive Personality...48

The Bum..50

Carnival 53

My Game 55

Me and Charlie 61

First Trip West 64

Back Home Looking at the Problem....................................66

A Look at Blackouts 68

About Journaling..75

See Who I Am...77

One Opinion 79

Score Somewhere 82

He Didn't Like Me, I Hated Him 84

Inmate on Tour 86
No More Family..93
Insanity Prevails...95
Another Felony 97
One Boring Sunday Night...100
Simple Insanity Turned Evil..102
Par for the Course 105
Rap Sheet 107
Always a New Job 109
About the Author 114

A Friend

*L*ong ago, in what was a much gentler time of life, a teenage boy walked into the life of our family. He was polite, well-mannered, and personable—just an all-around, clean-cut young man from the '50s era.

The adults in our family loved Mr. Personality, and of course, the kids who were all within three years of his age looked up to him. He was a role model to some and a big brother image to others. This future bad boy would take us for rides in his 1950 Mercury; he rode a motorcycle also. He would pick us up, if needed, most the time without too much of a grumble.

Rolled into the sleeves of his tee shirt would be a pack of cigarettes. His hair slicked back into a D.A. hairstyle. His hobby was working on cars to make them run well enough to get from point A to B most of the time. Then again, most from his era did the same. It was survival out of necessity. He learned how to survive in his later years.

His instincts were keen.

From time to time, you could find him playing solitaire while listening to rock and roll on the radio. He went to dances, as we all did. We all listened to forty-five records having Sunday family get-togethers at my aunts. It was part of our wonderful era. This young man was part of one of the best generations known to us. He was part of the '50s era, the typical all-American teenage boy.

He grew up within our family structure as he was dating one of the girls. We all grew up together for about six years—the most formative years for most teenagers. The youngest of this family unit was a boy who looked up to Mr. Personality as a role model.

Then the beginning of the end came. He married into our family. We, the kids of the family, were *thrilled* to have him as one of us. I was in the wedding; all the cousins were in the wedding. That's just the way things were—one big happy family!

I can't emphasize the word *family* enough. My point is that I want the readers to understand this young man before his downfall. He was a good person who happened to have bad things happen to him, not much later on in life, to be honest. Something called *alcohol* grabbed hold and wouldn't let go for a few decades. He survived as he always did. The young man our family knew was gone. We grieved his loss once the bottle took hold of his being and had a tight grasp on his body and soul.

This is a story of that young man's journey through life. Hopefully, as you read this, you will remember the clean-cut, nice young man I have described to you.

A Friend

Evolution

There is mention of a drinker crossing an invisible line into alcoholism. This average, if somewhat naïve twenty-year-old was stopped cold in the process of gaining knowledge and maturity. Life's lessons about fairness, goals, and devotion to friends and family weren't important then. This impressionable age has a lot of "hidden people" with many lives to live, if called upon. Behind the curtain was a raging alcoholic waiting to be chosen. Although dormant until that time, it stepped up armed to the teeth demanding total submission. The knowledge and understanding that comes with maturity and the love of life becomes forever unattainable. Now, it is *on with the show*!

There was a wedding I attended at age fourteen where I drank many draft beers and then once with a buddy at the age of seventeen and a half.

I was four months into being twenty years old when alcohol became my one and only desire. The drinking was only to get drunk, not socially, nor in any moderation. It wasn't really bad at first. Then it was more and more until it became an obsession. It was a constant desire that built a wall to keep everything else out. Alcohol was a king who demanded complete devotion—a very strong and dangerous master who would deceive by trickery and beat one into addiction. Then seemingly, I was handcuffed to it by the time I was twenty-one. I was so hooked! Not drinking every day, but of that mind-set. The hidden devil master was on the inside, grouping thoughts and mistakes to fire during the next kamikaze mission.

The show was good. When I talk about the show, I am referring to a life of partying. When the show crashed, it was horrible. Compelled and 98% percent regrouped, on with it! Another trick to remain ruler, the show got great. Another painful crash and regroup 97% of the 98% that was left and continue. On with the show, on with the crashes chipping away up to 40% of self-worth. Only today, the bottle and the constant sedation were of any importance.

I had no valid excuse for what I had become, which was a liar, cheat, and a thief. I was never a functioning alcoholic; holding a job was impossible. All that mattered when I finally could get up was my next drink. Then mostly in desperation, it didn't matter how just as long as I got my bottle. I became a moocher and a scourge to be avoided. I didn't care because people didn't matter. I knew what most of them thought of me, but I'd be on my way soon anyway.

Then came the trouble, the beatings (I only won a few fights), the jails, and the scroungiest places I never wanted to be in. The routine was to regroup and look for the next show, the drink. Always the show!

How Could this Happen

Much of this is not expected to be understood, as the writer can only guess at some of it.

There is much confusion in it all. This is written and lived as if there are two people. By definition, it is a type of psychosis characterized by loss of contact with environment and by disintegration of personality. Sure I got that out of a book, but that really seems to cover it! There can be no other reason why I did the things I did. I acted the way I acted out of insanity rather than by any rational behavior. If there was ever a good excuse, it would be found in the Bible in the New Testament, Romans 7:20, saying, " Now if I do what I will not to do, it is no longer I who do it, but sin that dwells in me."

To wake up to a bright day is still amazing to me. There is no simple way to change evil in a man who has an alcohol addiction. He is a liar, cheat, and a thief. He is irresponsible, selfish unreliable, and sometimes dangerous. With no specific treatment for it, I had to begin with what I learned in a twelve-step program. There were countless attempts at sobriety but apparently not ready to grow up yet.

So many years without a clue, then a spark of maturity to be drowned out again. Being free of drugs and alcohol was the key to a new beginning but it was hard to achieve, so prayer became a constant practice. It was still twenty years later before a beginning was established. If there was a price to be paid, it was in the years of conflict and turmoil, loss and much pain, in the tears and confusion. The strong hate that lived in me made it possible for evil to grow there also. There was so much in me that needed to change. I heard someone say in the meetings, "I didn't see the light. I felt the heat!" That had me thinking about tomorrow like I never did before. Where will I be? Where do I want to be?

It is very doubtful that anyone else thought the same way. Up to this day, I am so ashamed of most of the things I did. In the twelve-step program I had been involved with, there is a part that states "We do not regret the past nor wish to shut the door on it." " While most everything else is true this statement is the further most from "My Truth." How can anyone having done what I did not regret it? Only if done rationally and intentionally can one say he does not regret what he has done. This is not the case here. If I had it to do all over again, would I do the same thing? Of course not! Therefore, it is most regrettable even to admit these things.

It is true that most people would say that I am a good guy. Some would go as far as to say that I am humanitarian. That of course is one person they are describing. The other person who I became would not get the same description. That one would be full of distain—vulgar and disgusting! There was a time when I would cease to consider my actions as my own responsibility. All those horrid things would be on another person's conscience, not mine. Never did I think that I was responsible. Just because I was under the influence of a mind-altering drug, I was not liable. "It wasn't me" was what I told others, and that was my delusion. This went on for years. It wasn't my fault. I believed it and, at times, got others to believe it too.

So many times, I heard people say, "He's OK when he's sober." That only reinforced the belief that I was not responsible for my actions. That in itself is ludicrous, but that is what I believed. When I had to answer for these actions, I felt injustice. It wasn't me at the time. That is what I believed and nobody could make me believe my punishment was just or even deserved. Surely, I knew I was guilty but by reason of psychosis, I believed I was not liable. Therefore, in my own little mind, *I was not guilty*! The good guy would show up, and I got away with very much. When I was made to answer for my infractions, the good guy would receive the punishment when the schizoid should have. The judges—and I suppose people in general—saw these many personalities and had some compassion for me as a victim. I was a victim only of my own insecurity. Nothing else! What made me that way is debatable! Things can be pointed to, and/or blamed, but not held totally responsible. Yes, I do believe there were deciding factors. There were instances that aided in the irrational thinking that I was not liable. Sure this can be debated too. Some would believe there is definite assessment of responsibility; others would adhere only to the possibility.

Upon examining such a past over and over, I now know that only I am responsible. I am liable, and I alone deserve to carry this horrible guilt. I am the culmination of my past of course, but I do have many regrets, and I do wish to shut the door on it! Too bad! I can't.

Off to a Bad Start

*H*aving a problem with authority was evident in my school record—mostly for smart remarks to teachers that got me expelled three times in the eighth grade and I did not pass that year. Then with bad behavior, I got expelled again once in the eighth, ninth, tenth, eleventh, and twelfth grades.

I had the same girlfriend all through high school and got engaged when I graduated. A year later, we were married. No one could tell me otherwise. The marriage lasted four months. I never looked back and started drinking a little bit.

Bad attitude in the U.S. Army got me kicked out, but that was also by choice. Then I continued on with an aimless life. There was no inspiration ever. I actually looked for that from my father for years, but it never came. I only saw it in the movies. I was an adult before I saw how differently my own circumstances could have turned out. It seems that at least I would have learned not to be so impulsive. Without thinking things out first, many decisions were wrong ones. Although my thinking became distorted by addiction, many instances were just idiotic at best. This resulted in many misdemeanors: two felony convictions, a terrible motor vehicle record, and an undesirable discharge from the army. I even had a celebrity status with the younger crowd in town. Every time I got in trouble, it was put in the newspaper. I was looked at as trouble, a troublemaker, and a problem to be avoided.

Of course I didn't know this until years later. I couldn't handle all that trouble, but I suppose it was thought that I could. That was probably what kept me from getting beat up a few times. People were afraid of me, and I never knew it. That was not what I ever wanted but that was just the way it was. That was why I didn't need to fight very often. Whenever I did, I probably would have lost more than I won!

Most were quick ones except for the one that hurt me pretty bad. That one was provoked by my smart mouth to a big guy. Big mistake for sure!

I don't do that anymore but am sometimes inconsiderate of others. This is not intentional but out of absentmindedness. It is so easy to be taken out of context, but I am working on being more genuine. Like you've heard before, I am not yet who I want to be, but I'm glad I'm not who I used to be.

The best of my memory counted over 50 arrests, and more than 25 different jails in 9 states. There have been many debts paid to society through jail time and heavy fines, but I will carry the baggage of the past wherever I go.

In trying to figure out or make an excuse, it is easy to assign blame. Why was I the black sheep of the family? Maybe it was because I always did the wrong thing. I was the only one out of a family of seven kids! If you didn't know it already, neglecting a child is abuse. I was left to my own wanderings, bad choices, and decisions; I made a mess of things quickly. I was never taught anything, shown, or instructed except for the things I didn't want. My life consisted of church and playing an instrument, band practice, and school. I was "painted black" at a young age. Sometimes the butt of jokes, but the jokers were unaware of my ability to overlook most of it. I never wanted confrontation, so I let it ride, left it alone, and went on my way.

In all my years, I never saw a heated argument between my parents, but there was still trauma for me. It does not matter how old you are when these instances occur. You will remember trauma and disappointment!

My dad provided food and shelter but wanted nothing to do with me. Not even once in my memory. The way he catered to my younger brother let me see how different it could have been. I can't imagine what a little kid could do to make him ignore me the way he did, but it must have been something he may have been able to remedy. He was not interested. I hated that man every minute of my life. Although very difficult and took a very long time, I did forgive him after forty years. A lot of water under the bridge, but it can still be a hurt to experience. There are many reminders so I can't forget it. There are also some lingering resentments, but I am tougher now and it rolls off quicker.

Off to a Good Start

I came from a family of beautiful people, but for some reason, I was always the black sheep. This was way before I had the first drink, way before the trouble started, and way before the idiotic things I started.

From my first arrest, there was never anyone interested in bailing me out. Only $25.00 and I would have walked out of there. Forget about it because there isn't anybody coming. After that, whenever I got locked up, I wouldn't even call anyone. There were a lot of arrests so I did ask occasionally, but the answer was always a "Can't help ya!"

Even when the police planted a nickel bag of marijuana where I was staying in 1967, I was more innocent than the cops who were prosecuting me. That time, I stayed in the county for three weeks until my good friend from the carnival heard about it and came straight there to get me out. It was $1,000 bail, meaning $100 to a bondsman.

I got the same possession charge a year later for a bag that was in the glove compartment of the car I was riding in. That was another $1,000 with help from the same friend and the same bondsman. That was the beginning of a long relationship with this bondsman. He came to get me out a few more times after that.

Like I said, I did call family a few times, thinking maybe this time they'd help me. It never happened! You cannot imagine the hurt when you do not get any help from the only people you have. It is depressing enough to be in jail, but when you find out that people couldn't care less, well just imagine yourself there and you would have an idea how it feels. All of a sudden, the charges and what happens in court doesn't even matter.

People wonder why some guys commit suicide in jail. It happened in this one joint I was in, and this guy had his own reasons. There are many reasons why a guy might do it, but this one was highly addicted to a drug that he got from the system to help him get off heroin. Methadone, a heavy pain killer, is administered regularly at a clinic in the neighborhood and it causes an addiction as bad as that of heroin. This man was on what they call methadone maintenance. And without it, he was getting sicker and sicker. He told a sergeant that he would hang himself if they didn't give him methadone. He was told that they didn't give that at that jail, and he was dead the next morning. He tied himself up to the towel rack that was welded into the wall at chest level, folded his arms, and put his feet on the toilet. The end! That could be part of withdrawing from any habit. I had thought about it myself while I was in there a few times.

The one and only time my parents helped me out was on a Christmas day. I'd just left my two kids and their mother around Thanksgiving and went there to see them on Christmas Eve. The kids weren't there, and there was a party going on. I knew everyone there, even her new man. He was a big muscle dork from my hometown. Of course I was drunk and mostly irate because the kids weren't there and not because she had a new man—that part was no surprise at all.

I suppose I just wanted to be mad at something, so I pushed the Christmas tree over, breaking a lot of the decorations. Of course the mad woman took a swing at me, so I pushed her hard enough for her to go through the wall. I think that was the noise I heard. Then I was looking for the muscle man to jump, but he never moved. There was another guy there, and I think I slammed him, but I really don't remember all of it. I had a ride waiting for me so I left right after that.

It was a traditional Christmas day at my parents' house, having a big family gathering. They were all there, and I was just having a smoke while lying on my brother's bed when my mom came in crying. I thought someone did something wrong and I'd go straighten it out. She said, "The police are here for you! I walked out into the living room, and of course I knew them. I went to take a big hit on a bottle of whiskey when they said, "Take your time." You really don't need cops hanging around your house, so I took another big drink and hit the door.

This was some sort of an assault charge from the night before. So I went to jail—nothing new, right? I was only in a cell for about two hours that time. My father had gone to the bar where I spent most of my time and got two guys, who were both needle junkies, to show him how to bail someone out of jail. Little did he know, he was always so naive.

All the other small-time arrests and the small-time bail, but they never got me out before. I didn't understand it until my mother told me she didn't want to give my ex the satisfaction of having me in jail on Christmas day. There was another time when I was involved with an automatic weapon long before you could buy one on any corner. The bail was set at $25,000 with no 10%. I really thought I'd be down on that one for a while, but no, I got arrested on a Friday night and was walking Monday morning. At my arraignment were two of New Jersey's top criminal lawyers. That was a gift from a friend. There, I was granted the privilege to obtain a bondsman for the 10%. Much to my surprise, it was my sister and my brother-in-law who put up the cash before the arraignment.

This was in the papers for miles around, even a week later. All my drunk charges always made the local papers, but when I got a no bill on that one, it hit the front page. That meant they had insufficient evidence to prosecute me. Isn't it nice that I've learned all these things? There were many arrests after that one, but in jail was where I stayed!

Depression

If this depression cannot be overcome then it must be "the monster" to each and every one of its victims! It is no wonder the doctors are baffled by this because the problem affects their patients in different degrees or in different stages when they come in for treatment. People who are not severely hampered by this may say that since their first prescribed medication, they've been fine. The people who are totally encumbered by this are the only ones I see during an inpatient checkup. In a room full of people up against a terminal problem, this "thing" seems to take on such a presence. I mean you can almost see it! As the talk goes around the room, it is quite evident that these people are equally incapacitated. This is to the point of complete surrender to it. What got me to that point were the countless vain attempts at changing the anti-depressants over the years with no success. I can only guess at when it started because at first it was rare and brief. Some fifteen years later with almost that many medications and doctors, I still think about death sometimes. As for the people who are cured by the first medication, I believe a placebo would have the same result! These people I do not see because they do not make it to inpatient treatment. Hospital staff will refer to these groups of miserable people being asked to vent in front of strangers as treatment. Then there are simple instructions on how to cope. Maybe this is some first stage treatment. By the time we get there, I would imagine that most of us have tried those things. We are told to get a hobby, get busy, get involved, go for walks, write a journal, or simply talk to someone. This all does seem elementary, but nothing is mentioned as to where the desire will come from. When a depression is such debilitation that one will go into seclusion, there will be no hobby or anything else! There will be no housecleaning or washing dishes! There will hardly be a shave and a shower, or anything constructive! Rather, the mood is to destroy! Pretty much anything you do that takes your mind off it will help, but surrender usually takes precedence! I can only express my own view on this, but the isolation only comes after many vain attempts at a cure. The pain that the monster causes is not consistent throughout the day. It can ease up and return many times in the same day. This is when it is at its heaviest, but I have come out of this for some extended periods. It seems that when you have it this bad, it doesn't come back on gradually. Mostly a recurrence will be severe and sudden. Could a trivial problem trigger this or is it part of the monster that it can't be triggered by situational stuff? Yesterday I had a problem that I was able to walk away from with my serenity intact. I took notice of how well I handled the situation mentally.

Then at 4 a.m., a dream about this woke me up and it was on full force. With depression causing me insomnia, it is with much effort that I do anything. Again back to the only answer I know, isolation. This means quiet TV, reading, writing, or trying to sleep. This can go on for days with no enjoyment in any of it. During hospital detoxifications, depression is evident in most and it is to be expected at that time. There were some brief behavior modification talks, but they were pretty much overlooked while talking about alcoholism. It was many years later. I was approximately four years sober that I was admitted sober for depression alone. There they did what their instructors directed them to do and also would improvise where they could. With so many recurrences, why would I think another inpatient treatment would help? Inpatient treatment in itself is at least some protection from life's terms because of the controlled environment.

A Will to Survive

This of course is necessary to provide an open mind to any problem. I can appreciate a good start but all has failed miserably.

So many years *later* and still the same depression! It was compounded by the loss of a dear friend, who was also the love of my life. That was some sixteen months ago and more often than not, I miss her. I am saddened to the point of quiet tears. How is this dealt with? I suppose it isn't. I just live with it.

After a life of self will run riot by addiction, we will spend the rest of our lives in recovery. This is constant vigilance. There will be depression and loneliness as a residual effect on most addicts.

Whether clinical or situational, depression is best fought by staying busy. Keeping the mind occupied is the key. It does not matter what activity this is. It is only to stay out of self, where we always choose to dwell on the problem. It could be as simple as reading to take you away for a while.

The main difficulty here is taking action. The journey of eight thousand miles also ends with a single step and that is where we see ourselves! This is only after many attempts at finding happiness. Still, the instinct to survive is there so we persevere or try again. With the mood demanding inactivity, staying busy at the very least is a reluctant beginning. It is either halfhearted or short-lived with surrender always being an option. With distorted logic, the easy way always looks good.

When faced with an immoveable object, build around it. The thought is if it can't be beat, then take what you have and run with it. Suicidal is a horrible way to spend a day! You are always looking for an answer but always failing and giving up.

A tiny light at the end of the tunnel may bring a new inspiration. Having been so inspired prior to this, the new inspiration is coupled with skepticism and doubt. The comfort of surrender is always the safety net or plan B. We have found our way back to it before and have learned to live in isolation. This is protection from any new hurts. As the depression perpetuates, we become very fragile. This is why the isolation has such an appeal! Here, the situation will not improve anymore but it is the only serenity available.

This is undoubtedly "a screaming heartache" usually without any reason for it. I don't believe there can be a remedy if the cause is not apparent. Forever living on a prayer, will try again on the morrow!

The Monster

*T*his episode with the monster depression is the worst one yet because of the length of it. To think it is over when it isn't is a first. Out a little then back in. Light, then dark. Right now, I am thinking that isolation looks good. Even to go there willingly! The "cave" is what I call it. At times I cannot go there yet I feel it is the best armor I have.

Today I will not go anywhere. I think I need a rest from this. I will not worry and try not to fear these demons. I will not even think if I can. This could all be positive, at the same time points to the sanctuary of the cave. It certainly has its lure, and I am now usually drawn to it. This is only a temporary serenity. I get a break from it but it comes back on like the same truck running over me again. Seems the blow is only lessened because the wound is already there. I may be learning something but surely not defenses.

OK. This gets heavy so pay attention! An in-depth look at the situational stuff would consider a logical depression to the degree of the situation. How long it lasts and our reactions will be different, but as I see it, circumstances will demand a certain depression. This is logical; not a news flash! This is just looked at as untreatable. Some people get tranquilizers. For me, this has never been suggested *unless* each and every contributing factor in this malady is considered. How possible is an accurate concept of the problem? It has been my observation that an inaccurate diagnosis and remedy will not only prolong, but intensify the problem. Elementary yet baffling!

Only by Faith can Inspiration Come from Inadequacy

Most of the hospital stays are preceded by countless attempts at rectifying the situation. It is so hard to ask for help not knowing what help is. Inpatient treatment is the last resort, repeated failure diminishes hope. Hope doesn't last long. The white flag comes out and I go back to the cave to hurt in private. There is sanctuary but no security with anger.

As the causes and effects in two types of depression are different, so is their arrival and departure. Together they are first the monster. Even with countless failures as learning experiences, I doubt any defense has been established. Many are the professionals that have studied this and right along with them are the patients. There has been much trial and error and many studies. There are millions still clueless!

We hear words of encouragement from nonprofessionals like "Keep your chin up," "Just look around you," and the like. These are good for situational sadness, not the monster!

There is no escape from the monster. This time everything is different: the warning before the crash, the extent of the isolation, and the complete defeat before getting somewhat better then wake up worse. Good mornings usually magnify themselves as do bad ones, so whatever mood I wake up to will be my day!

The worst part of what is different this time is how it can let up considerably and then crash again. When it lets up gradually, you believe it is about to subside, but it comes back. Now, the quick flip makes me think about bipolarity, but I don't think about it much. (I don't understand it and have only seen the upside.) Not as bad as it gets right now for days. I have been experiencing a pain that comes prior to and during crying. Believe me, tears from a straight face is no relief. That inner pain is screaming soundlessly! I mean it is physically painful!

The Serenity Prayer works for me and can be empowering. Also for me, the best one to ask for help is the *great physician*. I still believe *He* will provide an answer, as I become more apt to recognize it.

Treatment is only a new pill while in patient for observation. They wish you good luck, and give you an appointment in three months. It never works.

I have severe depression today! Another payment on the long-gone show, as I sit here miserable for the past few weeks.

Yesterday was better for about an hour but returned to crash site. Anyone who knows me could see at a glance that I am very troubled. I am not living near anyone who knows me and I sit quietly in my locked apartment to hide from my neighbor buddies. In all my depression I do not seek medication to cure logic. This past year I lost three people I cared about, and some other stuff, and this caused a depression; that is logical. This is very similar in darkness but not in origin! These two different types of depression when coupled are lengthier. I am not strong enough in my heart for this. Maybe I will live in my own hell until every debt is paid. Circumstantial and recorded evidence points in that direction. Over the years, I've prayed and cried until I almost self-destructed. The Bible says, "To those that have much, more will be given. To those that have little, even what they have will be taken away." If I understand correctly, this tells me that I was created without a chance to succeed. To look at me, you can't see my sin, nor can you see what I have done to pay what I owe. I have paid a lot, but will the debts ever be paid off? I am so exhausted! All I have right now is little hope and that is rare. Undoubtedly you have heard suicide referred to as the cowards' way out. Specifically that is true. More so, how would anyone know? What you see is not exactly what I get. All the hurts are not obvious, nor is a voiced complaint. I carry around much more than even my mother could see. She has always had good solutions for me but I no longer burden her serenity with my lack of it. As with most cases of depression, I sit alone in my misery. Years go by and I am still the same. I wake up in the morning and wish I hadn't. Those days are long, painful, and empty. This has been severe for years, basically always alone with the problem except for the medications. I don't think anyone is always depressed. Are the medications working then, or not needed? When terribly depressed are they no match when really needed? There is no answer. I am in a darkness you wouldn't believe. It is demobilizing, debilitating, and degenerating. It just gives me a bad attitude and that is a terrible distortion of who I really am. These days are very long and I look forward to the night when I can take the sleeping pills that don't always work. Then don't get too excited about tomorrow either, because it ain't over till it's over! It is true that I am mean sometimes and then back to isolation. The lights are low in the back bedroom. The sound of the small TV is low, and I am hiding There is no way out so just leave me alone. *Please*!

Get Some Help

After many near-death experiences, if you are fortunate you land in "the rooms" of a recovery program. What you hear and what you learn there from others is experience, strength, and hope. Quietly observing, you see many miracles and after a while you can even predict some of the falls. The seemingly small things we talk about can have a profound effect on someone you don't even know. The same as what you yourself will realize at times. There is no magic to this! That is why it is recommended to keep coming back. There is no graduation day ever! It is suggested to us that we put as much into recovery as we put into addiction. We can go to the bar. We can get to the meeting. Having no car when it's raining never stopped us before. No whining either. Sit in that chair and don't say much more than your name until your sponsor asks you if you have something to say. It doesn't always go that way, but when you are in new recovery, it is suggested that you just listen. Addiction is always waiting for you, and all you need to do is pick it up. The addiction is progressive even after you stop. When you pick it up again, it is worse, as if you never stopped. Well yeah! We knew that, but not how bad it could get so fast. Then after another episode, we wonder what happened. This is the same with most all of us. It is a malady from a hell that you don't ever want to know, *ever*!

Stay around long enough and you will realize the joy in those rooms where there was once the most pitiful human being. This is a taste of something many of us have never known. After the cloud nine wears off, and it better, we learn to face life on life's terms. This is something new to us all. Many bumps are in the road ahead but there is also a clean life to look forward to.

Some find religion after recovery. Others find recovery after they find a God of their own understanding. It is my own belief that whichever one you start with will ultimately lead you to the other! This, of course, is if you don't leave before the miracle. We collectively believe that these are truly miracles because there is absolutely no simple cure. Look at what he was and look at what he is now. You, yourself would agree that God is in this somewhere.

About Alcoholism
and Depression

Alcoholics come in all shapes and sizes. They are not the much thought of skid row types only. Last I heard those unfortunates make up about 3% of us. Some have an inexhaustible bank account or a source of income which I'm sure contributes to their problem. Others sometimes will only stop drinking because they have no money. Then it becomes a struggle to find the money needed to alleviate their sickness in the morning, then a bit more to find whatever is necessary for the rest of the day. For this the addict will summon all the wit, lies, and promises to get the job done. There are resolutions and plasma donations; they will sell the TV, pawn anything they have or whatever it takes to get the bottle or drug and often enough both! Once this is accomplished, we can go to the park and relax. If we have a place to stay, we can go there and try to think of how this can be done again the next day. It ain't over till it's over, and it's never over! This is insidious behavior, but with addiction, it is the only way.

Of course it is different with the functioning addict. There is always a payday. There are no blood banks, no scroungy bars, and not much borrowing or stealing, if any. What remains forever present are the lies Why you were late for an appointment, late coming in from work, totally absent when needed, where the money went, and mostly lying about the things you did that are too shameful to admit. Over a period of time, these character defects become so embedded in a life style that they become permanent. For a period of time, one may escape the malady just to prove a point, to satisfy a spouse, a place of employment or a judge, but the character defects remain. There is an analogy about a drunken horse thief. Take away the booze and you still have a horse thief. This makes it quite evident that once your system is cleaned out, your thought patterns leave much to be desired.

This is just the beginning of a long thought process of changing. During addiction only self is of any importance. Sure there are other concerns but only after the addict's needs are met. If this takes longer than expected, there is no time for anything else and you will just have to understand. If you don't, and you most likely won't, then too bad for you!

The addict is the most selfish person. Addiction will not permit any variance. It is all about me satisfying myself. If I have any time to give of myself, I may as long as nothing interferes with my own priorities. If anything or anyone has to be stepped on to accomplish this, so be it! I will walk over you to get where I need to be. If I can't come back to help you and you are finished with me, then that is looked at as part of the price we had to pay and accepted as just that. If I got my fix at your expense, too bad for you. Apparently, you didn't see the importance of my dilemma. Therefore you were against me, and any friendship we may have had was looked at as no great loss. This, in itself, is one of my biggest regrets. There were so many people I took advantage of or beat in one way or another. Some of these folks were really good people, but my addiction came first. I could have had good friends in these people but squashed any further association. There are no do-overs There were some second chances but addiction won out every time.

Then there may be a moment of clarity, a spiritual awakening if you will. There is a fellowship with others that were once so enslaved; you begin to see the malady that your addiction really is.

While in treatment, an alcohol counselor suggested we write a letter to our addiction that may put together what we evidently could not put together in our own minds at the same time. A little at a time, I began to write. Seeing just what I had been dealing with, I was able to see how my weak attempts at recovery were futile.

So I began:

Dear Addiction,

How you must miss me! Didn't we go everywhere together? From the very first flake, I took you off the shelf. Then it really snowed! Three inches, three feet, six feet and buried, you were all over me and I loved you so much. No matter what we did or where we went, you had me covered. You kept me warm, showed me how to dance and sing, and even made me some kind of combination of Don Juan and King Kong. I could even drive better. I had more fun with your other lovers, and you were everywhere I was.

Then you started taking me to places I didn't want to go. You scared off every friend I could have had. You made my own kids hate me. You cost me every job I ever had and took every dollar I ever had. I'll never have my own home or a new car. You caused me to be mean, ugly, dirty, and unable to care about anything else. You made me callous, unable to love or go to church and other places you weren't welcome. Whenever I left you, I always took you back expecting you to be different. You only got worse and made me more evil. I took you back many times after doing well without you and still you got worse. Although you are the master of disguise, you only deceive by trickery. When I found others you did this to, I joined them in an honest effort to keep you away. Now guess what? When all your exes are together you can't touch us! You can only bully the helpless; but when we are together, you are powerless.

If we could only get in between you and your new ones, you'd never have another. You know we can't do that, but you can be sure we will be there to catch them when they fall.

You are dead! I am not! Good-bye!

Thank you very much, but this time it only lasted a year.

With most addicts, it is the family and friends that see the problem first. After a lot of irrational actions in all the places we would frequent, we became known as people to avoid. We can be too loud and ignorant of the present situation, making jokes of a serious matter. This is when others first see the effects with the immediate personality change. Sometimes aware of the ass we made of ourselves, we'd find another place to drink. After a while, the same thing would happen and it would be off to the next place where we were not known. This happening as often as it did, many of us become loners. This is better because the new crowd doesn't know yet what an ass you're apt to be.

Then you are alone most of the time. You live alone with no company other than the nearby drinkers who drink the same way. If you're anything like me, even these folks will put some distance between you and them after they've had enough. When completely shut out by everyone, the attitude is that you are just not understood. "These people are all wrong about me," is what you tell yourself. "Everyone is wrong and I'm right!" You really do believe this.

If you refuse to change, you will be alone like never before and sometimes this is so horrible. The loneliness will drive you to the bottle just to escape the feelings. You come out of it in the morning and nothing has changed, but the bottle is empty. I believe that alcohol and drugs are nothing more than "escape-ism." All the fun is out of it and to become emotionally numb becomes your only relief! Living alone with the habit, the depression, and the anger is one horrible place to be. There were many days that I wanted to get violent at almost anything or anyone. My reason being that life wasn't worth living anymore. Caught up in my own trap, I had so many problems that the last thing I thought would help me was to put the bottle down. I would continue to drink while I got my life back in order. It took a long time to realize that nothing would get in order until I got sober. Then things would fall in place but not until I get sober. It took a long time to get to where I was, and it would take some time to mend the wreckage of my past.

Quite a while in depression, every day gave me a reason to be angry; maybe not a logical reason but enough to keep me right where I was. This went on for a long time. Here was one of those days:

Seemingly held captive in my own prison, I looked out the window and saw a plane fly by and wish I were on it, or maybe in one of the cars going by to the store, the post office, an event, or just a ride somewhere. At the same time, I wouldn't go if I were asked; it will usually take a while to realize this captivity, and coupled with situational hurts, it is frustration from the start. I never did enjoy being indoors. I would like to be out and about but I just couldn't. I had things to do, but no matter the regard, the penalty for being late, or the lost opportunities, I just couldn't go anywhere. All people, places, and things just tend to irritate me.

The next day I still have stuff to do, but once in a while there is a physical immobilizer. Later in the day, I get dressed and start for the door, but usually will sit back down to drink more coffee until I am ready. Then the mood changes; I change my plan and go nowhere.

First thing in the morning is the worst time. This is the same as waking up in a jail and realizing where you are. You become very irritable and fragile. While hurting and looking for an answer, there is occasional worry, planning, and maybe a new idea with a lot of giving up in between. It always reverts to "never mind, there is no answer!"

I had just arrived home from a twelve-day hospitalization for treatment of depression. I was discharged with no progress. I had not had a drink in four years. Par for the course, there was another change in medication. I never saw any importance in keeping records, nor does it matter how many I've been on. If there really was an answer, there wouldn't be so many choices. After such a lengthy inpatient treatment, I came home worse than when I went in. I don't blame anyone for not having an answer; first of all because they don't have all the contributing factors to accurately determine causes and effects.

The day begins with a pot of coffee and a lot of cigarettes, then more coffee and cigarettes. There is no appetite at all until late at night when the coffee wears off. I'd been told that eating healthier would make me feel better but after two weeks of eating well in the hospital, I saw no boost in energy. There was no coffee in there so I ate.

Some days, there is total absentmindedness. The concentration is brief at best, like walking towards the store in the door putting me closer to the lottery machine but I forget to get my numbers when I get in there. Remembering what I forgot will intensify the anger.

This is most of the way it was—monotonous, cruel, sad, lonely, angry, tired, and frustrated. Then one day you wake up and the sun is shining. Where did the depression go? No one can tell you that anymore than they can tell you where it came from.

Can there be one clear-cut remedy for all addicts? I think not! Having frequented many treatment facilities, I have seen many methods. Most of this treatment is administered by recovering addicts. There is nowhere in the book of Alcoholics Anonymous stating that "some are sicker than others," but it is heard often enough. Well this is surely so! This only stands to reason with all sorts of problems presenting themselves in the same room.

These "sicker than others" people are in treatment, and they are also on the staff in most places. Do you really think any one of us is ever cured totally when we are talking about insanity, mood swings, and bad impulsive behavior? My perception is that this is most common in all of us.

OK, A few days of initial recovery and you start hearing about what you need to do. People will tell you what happened to them and maybe the same can help you. Another counselor will suggest something different and both will work. At the right moment, almost anything is a good idea next to what we had been doing, and will work for all it's worth. Not so surprising, but what it is, is people you are taking advice from.

Over the years I've been around many psychiatrists and "certified" alcohol counselors with all sorts of credentials on their walls and years in business. The doctors make the biggest mistakes; overprescribing mostly because they never have enough time with you to do more.

Many of the counselors you will see at some twelve-step meetings, and there may be a topic wherein they are as baffled as anyone else.

These groups are mostly empathy personified. Hang around long enough and you really get to know people. What? Yeah! They get to know you too! So when you see these " certified" people still having trouble, you learn more about how we are all the same in many respects like the doctors and their questionable expertise.

Just keep looking for your own answers. When you are meant to have them, the teacher will appear. After that, there will be more questions, and in time new teachers.

All these twelve-step groups or self-help groups will always have many people with something to say. I believe that the smarter you are, the more people in the crowd you can learn from. Well duh! It is just that it has taken me a long time to learn how to listen!

Besides hearing, the dictionary says that listen also means yield to advice.

Most people will eventually meet someone and be in love. They get married or not, and live happily after. With the addict, this is not what usually happens. Yes we do meet people and are in love but the addiction alters whatever may have been. It will cause irreconcilable differences that lead to breakups.

In all the womanizing, I may have gotten lucky more than once finding the right women for me. These were ruined like everything else that was good in my life. This all brought me to where I am now, living alone. I have for many years.

Never a real moneymaker, my escapades led me to the pawnshop, or I'd sell whatever I had for the next "outing." Mostly all I have is secondhand stuff. I have many photos of family, people, and places. These are my treasures.

These knickknacks and stuff bring me a lot of "visits" from days gone by. This is good especially in the winter when I am inside most days. This is not how a man was meant to live but the solitude is great!

When things are not so bad (the mood I guess), my pictures and knickknacks will brighten my day. I will look at a picture of somewhere I've been and it absolutely brings me back there. Sometimes weird things happen like just putting on a pair of suspenders my dad gave me and glancing at a picture of him with them on. I'd never noticed it before that. There is a piece of a carnival game and some good memories, and then there are the things my girl left me. These make me laugh and they make me cry. Yeah!

The loneliness will come and then this is not where you want to be! Now that I am sitting here with all my memorabilia, I get so angry I feel like hammering everything I look at. I want to put a dumbbell through the TV screen, flip over the table, and punch the mirror.

In all the time I had to be in jail I learned how to do time. That is exactly what I'm doing in my own apartment when I'd rather not be here or anywhere. When the depression hits you, life and everything in it is worthless. All my "treasures" serve only to remind me of what I no longer have in my life. Then they hurt me!

While trying to see a way out of the darkness, the light seems to be swallowed up, leaving the sun high above. There's stuff around me; objects and items I can't describe. Turmoil, panic, and confusion followed by a complacently due to many priors. Then more hurt, remorse, and self- pity mixed with a survival instinct. I am in the garbage can!

My track record assures me that these are "days of future past." Exactly as written by the Moody Blues, it will happen again for sure.

These are just dead days I put in the bank years ago while at "the show." Sometimes it becomes easy to wallow in, if allowed and also easier to understand when realizing this is the bed I made, and a debt is being paid.

"On with the show" is just a colloquialism I use referring to my aimless behavior; not to be confused with the carnival known as show business to some.

Paying for a long-gone show, I am ever reminded of how costly being aimless really is! There are so many bad experiences to look back on when one gets sober for a while. The average person having been through these nightmares would make damn sure nothing like that would ever happen again, but not the alcoholic!

Alcoholism tells you that you don't have a problem and secondly that you can do the same thing and expect different results. It never gets better, only worse. Part of the insanity of alcoholism is to not believe what it is telling you. Time after time of trying to drink like a normal person and failing miserably, you still won't believe it and try again. You promise yourself that it won't happen again but there is always another catastrophe. Then the idea of controlled drinking sets off another succession of defeats. Trying to control your drinking is a sure sign that your drinking is out of control. Failure after failure, you still believe you can make it work. This goes on and on. Eventually you realize that this will never work, so you give up any attempt at control and go full blast. This will go on until it has run its course. At some point, you finally admit that there is a problem. This of course will not stop you either! As your life gets progressively worse, you begin to think that maybe something can be done. After another terrible experience, you decide to try to get help. By this time you are so beaten down that it takes a hospital detox. Even with the medication they give you to prevent any seizures and delirium tremors, it is still hell to go through. After a few days, your appetite comes back and you eat better than you've eaten in quite a while. Your feeling of wellness comes back, then you believe what alcoholism tells you that wasn't too bad. Everyone and anyone else can see that you were only part of a man, but the insanity of it tells you that you are all better and can drink safely because you are so healthy now. This is a lie you are perfectly willing to believe. What you want more than anything else is to drink and get away with it. Well it ain't gonna happen!

Maybe your first detox or first twenty-eight-day program and with your first taste of sobriety, you land on some sort of cloud nine. You absolutely think you are free at last; free at last from the physical need for a drink. Before this, you had to drink or you'd be sick and now you have a choice. If you are like most, after a while alcoholism will tell you that you are capable of having a drink without getting drunk. You may have a few to reaffirm that belief, then do it again until it gets worse. If you are lucky, you might make it back to treatment to try again. Some don't make it past a car wreck, or maybe a suicide. We don't all make it back!

For me there were many hospital visits—some in New Jersey, Las Vegas, California, and New Mexico. Although very sick, these were at least humane. The bad ones were when I got locked up and had to cold turkey detox. One minute you're hot and then you're cold. Along with practically vibrating out of my shoes, I called it "shake and bake." In a few hospital detoxes, I met some heroin addicts that become alcoholic and had a harder time trying to quit, saying it is a worse kind of detox. I only did heroin once after being dry for six months and was bored. I thought it was a good idea at the time. It wasn't!

Most places where one may go to detox will point you towards a twelve-step program. Yeah, yeah! That's for other people. That's for the ones who are not as smart as me or as healthy as the great me. You still think you don't need help..

Then it's back to jail for another drunk driving charge or any one of the many fiascos waiting out there for you. There isn't any telling because the human being is the most unpredictable animal, and the alcoholic is at the head of the call in that respect. Friends and family will distance themselves after repeatedly trying to help. In progression you are more alone than ever before. Even after a crowded bar where you think you had a good time, you begin to realize you will always suffer from the same loneliness.

Moral Defect

Whether you want to stop drinking or not, from time to time you will be without. To detox from alcohol more comfortably, you will need a small amount every three or four hours or you will experience different kinds of sickness. Some at the same time and some come and go.

In a hospital setting, you have the medication so it is easier, yet all the while most uncomfortable. Even with a vitamin B_{12} shot, you may not eat for a couple of days. Some places may give you a pill to help you sleep but compared to the heavy habit you have, this little pill will never work.

Depending on your youth and overall health, after a few days you will be able to sleep better and you develop a voracious appetite. Soon you feel good enough to look at where to go from here.

Totally different is to detox without the medications. If you have been there before, just knowing what will happen is depressing because with this, you know exactly how sick you are about to get. Stopped abruptly when going to jail all the time was always bad. This was a cruel way to go because of the food and the conditions mostly. The sickness comes on the same at home if you're detoxing cold turkey. I think that is in reference to how your own skin feels like when you are not sweating bullets. Most immediate are the nightmares and the insomnia. Before what I did was wake up drunk so the sickness was avoidable for a while.

Then came the hallucinations: monkeys running around the house, bugs crawling all over me, and people so real I talked to them until they disappeared. Whatever the alcohol hurt is now letting me know it needs more by hurting me back. There are these abdominal pain and headaches because you haven't eaten in a while and when you try to vomit, dry heaves give no relief. You are now a bit more physically spent. You only get catnaps because some idiotic dream wakes you up. You just want to pass out but you can't. You are not scheduled to be hungry for a while and sometimes even a small glass of water can make you sick. Back on the bed to make you suffer physical pain and the agony of mental anguish in the form of embarrassment, remorse, financial woes, legal problems, and fear of what else may be found. I get nauseous again, but dry heaves only make me tear up some more. A few times, even two days after my last drink, I hardly had strength to maintain balance enough to walk.

It takes time to get all of this sickness off, but the mental anguish is great. It may be necessary for the guilt to start the remorse that becomes the serious resolve to fix the problem.

This will last as long as it does. When feeling healthy and capable, we will do it again and again. Before long, we are as strung out as before. We don't see it getting worse ever time, but it does get worse every time!

You are on a merry-go-round and you don't want to get off; you can't get off! If you don't stop, one of three things will happen: you will be institutionalized, you will die, or you will go to prison. There are no other alternatives! Some people never get sober.

Long Recovery Period

The 12-step program that I belong to states, in part, that we should not regret the past! It would seem that the people who wrote the plan never did anything they wished they hadn't. That's very nice, and I'm sure they were just pleasant to be around. Then why did they need a self-help group?

All the drunks I've ever known, myself included, have done many regrettable things and some of these things are too terrible to forget or dismiss. Yes, I understand the principle, " Pick up the pieces and live for today," but today is so badly marred by yesterday that regret is ever present! Some of the depression is due to the guilt and shame of it all, is constant and firmly planted right now. It all ties in so how do I ever let go?

It took years to get here and it will take all the years I have left to undo some of it, all the while making adjustments to live with whatever can't be repaired.

The way it works for me is that some of the things I did can be undone but the things I didn't do cannot be done at present or ever. Regret is not the only thing that is detrimental to my chance at serenity, but it is there and always will be!

This is just more "paying for the show" that the curtain closed on long ago. Somewhere in recovery you will hear someone say, "You have to do this yourself because no one will do it for you." This may be true, so you find out where you can get help, making it doable. Taking suggestions from people and programs provides an abundance of help, and when you put your dependence on a proven plan of action, you really don't do it alone. The truth is you can't anyway!

You may have had the strength to drive past a liquor store, but it is where you got that strength from that is more responsible for the victory! The determination comes from you wanting a change, but the strength comes from the twelve steps and more clean time.!

Looking back over the years of bouncing in and out of a recovery program, I can now see how the depression was responsible for most failures. This may come from a deliberate submission to the addiction, nonetheless a failure! A severe depression makes recovery all but impossible! This is like trying to blow up a balloon with a hole in it. The "big balloon" of recovery is killed by a tiny hole! You can try and you can make progress, but you won't succeed! The doctors with the medication do nothing for the hole in the balloon. They merely devise new ways to blow it up? This will place dependence on a failing plan, creating a malady of its own.

This simple analogy can show you how recovery is made possible by fixing one thing. The process is slow and many of us are fragile during this time. Every little upset may not send one back to the addiction, but it can pave the way!

Looking back at the days of addiction and turmoil, I think of how difficult it was just to get to the store for the day's supply. Whether capable or not, this was a mandatory trip! Always looking like death, I'd throw on a coat and hat to hide some of what I looked like and go for it. It was always a good feeling to get back with a new plan for the day. Maybe I would live after all. In an hour or so, my sickness would wear off and I'd be good. As good as it gets anyway! That was good enough for me! It wasn't really very good, but as long as I had my booze, cigarettes, and lottery tickets for the night I was comfortable.

Food was not a big concern at all. Maybe I'd eat later! That later got me to be thirty pounds underweight and incapable of walking. My one and only ambulance ride to the hospital and I 'd be detoxed. I was sicker then I knew, as they put me on the medical floor to get me well enough to go to the detox. That was for about a week or so and I was right back at it. Back then I could bounce right back, but later there was no bounce left. It got worse every time!

So many similar stories tell us that it takes whatever it takes before we clean up. Some go insane and some even die. I have been privileged with a way to recover.

There was so much to be discovered; things that had always been there, simple pleasures in life I'd never been able to appreciate like the beauty of a tree. Did the whole world around me change its appearance? No! I just had new eyes in my perception of it all. This was all new and exciting until the newness of it wore off. This is the cloud nine most of us experience with newness at sobriety. Soon after, I learned that this is not where you want to be. We need to take it slow, level off, and easy does it one day at a time. We learn and then fail! Learn some more and fail some more is what most of us had to do before ever being successful at sobriety. Then in time things do get better. We learn from our mistakes and the mistakes of others we've come to know. One really new thing to me is that I now have feelings I never had before. As I take better care of myself, I am better willing and able to lend a hand if needed. I have come to enjoy helping others. This is not only in recovery but in everyday life!

This is not all fun and games for us. It is a daily reprieve from a hell you can't imagine. Never forgetting where you came from will help. That is why we hear about keeping the memory green. You will remember your last drink or you may not have had it yet.

Then there is the part about not all days being good ones. Well, welcome to the real world! No whining allowed! Hold on to what you've got and make it through the day no matter what. This too shall pass. Yeah? I know! It is just that patience is something that none of us ever have. To an extent, we could all work on that one. Some days are brutally cruel, but how could we appreciate the sun if it never rained?

There is so much to be gained in recovery—it is no less then amazing. The many fears of people, places, and things are no longer a problem for us. We can face the day with expectations and even strength when needed.

We can feel good about what we are doing. This in itself is *another miracle!*

43

Another Attempt

With a lifetime of drunken irresponsibility, new sobriety brings about problems I am not prepared for. Responsibility means holding a job, paying rent on time, balancing a checkbook, etc. It is as if I am a newborn adult, as if it's my first year and I have no experience. Some problems are not so serious but I was still not prepared. Depression is ignored in order to simply function.

Today is another bad day! I just cannot handle some of these days so isolation is the safety net.

I have asked for help in all the wrong places. I am immobilized by this depression again. I may be a bit lazy but I have no direction. There is never a change on the horizon, so why reach for it? I am constantly trying to hide the real me. I am in such a state that I don't want anyone to see me. This is a big part of why I always choose to isolate. When I was young, all I could see of "the show" was the good thing it could be. There are many possibilities, errors will be made, and there are dire consequences. Although you can't avoid what you can't see, from a distance this kind of life has a predictable end.

I have sat in church quietly trying not to cry throughout the whole service. On my way out, I doubt anyone noticed but the minister. This was long before I joined the church and became acquainted with most of the congregation. He could see my mood and told me to go and see him. Maybe he gave me some direction, but mostly what he told me was not to give up and keep trying. Of course this was good advice but not real help.   Whatever kind of help you have, they must not be reluctant in any of it. That kind of help is nil. Then we go elsewhere again! Most of these days are run without any energy or enthusiasm. I am always ready to give up. There is a lot of giving up before the last one, suicide. This would be obvious if investigated, but usually only realized by others with the expertise of hindsight.

Thinking about the one bullet in the revolver, it is 5:1 odds you pull the trigger on an empty barrel. Life is not worth living prior to this, so it is 5:1 that it will get worse. These thoughts come while in a dark mindset, making the solitude a contributing factor to the problem.

Suicide is an act. Being suicidal is a way of life! To see how serious you are about it, a doctor will question your method. This is to see how much thought you've given to this. Other than to determine true intent, questioning method is irrelevant.

Being in dire straits is a constant, but money can only make me more comfortable in my misery. It can't buy me out of it. I can see no possible end after years of failed attempts to correct the problems with medications.

Suicidal

Years of failure helped to develop a depression that was temporarily relieved by alcohol. Then years of alcohol abuse helped to develop a more severe depression—each feeding off the other while causing more problems. With alcohol being such a strong depressant, could it keep you depressed long after it is out of the system? Quite possibly! Deep regret will also bring on the depression so I suppose that's why it isn't recommended.

Depression is usually coupled with a sleep disorder; the mild additives they put in some antidepressants help with that at times. When there is sleep depravation, anger will intensify. This is the worst thing that can happen when trying to overcome a problem. With the anger comes frustration and confusion. You believe you are giving it your best, and when someone in your life fails to appreciate this, you become fragile and your feelings get hurt easily. Thinking someone put a hole in your balloon, you might just give up and do at times.

I have quit so many jobs, left so many places, and deserted so many people that I'm almost surprised I have the one good friend I do have. Roommates in the hospital with our different problems, we became friends while considerate of each other? Deal. I guess I was still trying to learn how to be somebody's friend.

When my world is in dilemma, I have a very bad attitude. I am mad at the world and people just irritate me in general. This is constant

46

and will only change on occasion. Sometimes I try to "fix it," but I usually don't. I could care less!

There were times when suicide had its appeal—on the fence between a good life and a good death and not being able to choose. Could be I am afraid of both.

A story line you may have seen in a movie is a priest or family member trying to persuade a man not to jump off a bridge. So you suppose the man just woke up that morning and made a decision? It isn't likely! It takes research. Other avenues are explored, methods and consequences or a note. The soul you see on TV standing on a bridge railing, the train tracks with a gun to his head has gone over this in his mind many times AS A SOLUTION!

So it would seem that with life's answer at hand, namely suicide, he would be less miserable than he's been in years. This explains the laugh or the smile as they go!

Addictive Personality

There is something called an addictive personality. This means that whatever you like, you like it a lot. It only seems to reason that if this is demonstrated in a child, addictions are a good possibility later on in life. If you do recognize this trait in a child, my opinion would be to closely look at what he or she throws himself into. Even a slight obsession would point to the said personality. The adult primarily responsible for that child should be prepared to investigate certain issues pertaining to the possibility of later addiction.

Knowing myself to be of that mind, I have turned down offers of drugs because I knew if I liked it, I'd have a problem with it. On the brighter side, if you don't get involved with it in the first place, you are victorious without the battle. Besides, I already had a habit!

It is believed that as innocent as marijuana is, it will lead to other drugs. This is true if you think "if this one is good the others should be also." If you try one, you are apt to try another but I believe that this would be an experiment you were going to try anyway.

There are so many drugs out there that will get you high, but when you already have an addiction to one, you will dabble. The others will always come in second.

My addiction was always more important than holding any one of the jobs I could have retired from by now. There were always too many geographicals. That is a change of address.

These were always somewhat exciting because it was a new arena. Of course, out the window goes any stability, accumulation of possessions, a sense of belonging, longtime relationships, and most of any serenity. If you brought the addiction with you, the hustle is the same everywhere!

How did I get here? Seemingly at a destination, there is so much to remember about the journey. The mechanic can recall every bolt; the climber can recall every crevice. Well, overcoming obstacles and getting a job well done is not always the case.

The "here" that I've created is not such a good place, nonetheless a temporary destination. Remembering all that got me here is like all the bolts (I twisted off) and all the crevices I (should have) used. It all makes me wonder just how dumb I was.

Unless you are perfect, retrospect will always show even the slightest of errors in a ruined life. Maybe I should have moved a bit slower and been a bit more taciturn? Had I done that in the past, my here and now would not be as it is. Quick moves and a sharp tongue were called for, just not as often as I thought.

Well, here I am anyway! What would I rather be doing? What would I do with a little money? What would make me most happy? I don't even know. Where would my new "here and now" be? What would I like to be doing? I'm still not sure! My one aim now is just to have serenity in the midst of what I cannot change! There are so many possibilities that could have made my here and now much worse. How I emerged somewhat unharmed I don't know, but I will always be grateful for that. OK! I should be thankful for what I have and relax, but for me that is not so easy. I may seem like a scatterbrain because wherever my mood is, it will not remain so for long.

Probably the greatest of help for me after I wallowed in self-pity for a while was what my mother taught me years ago. She always told me, "Just look around you!" We all will surely have problems but mine will always fade in comparison. Then there is a new hope on the horizon!

The Bum

Fort Dix, they said! That's where I would do basic training for a three-year hitch in the U.S. Army. I had just gotten six motor vehicle tickets and thought the army needed me. They didn't! After going through three article 15s, a special court martial, and seventy-four days of a six months' sentence in the Fort Dix Post Military Stockade, I was undesirably discharged. You could say we weren't in agreement so I initiated the discharge procedure. I quit!

I went back home to start anew. It was the Beatles Revolution! Everything was changing big time. All I ever knew was conformity and absolutely no individuality! That's just the way it was. This was a new thing and I liked it. I had no strings. My four-month marriage before the army netted no children so I stayed at Mom and Dad's until I could get my own place (in and out for about twenty-five years).

If I had a job I'd have some spending money. I never paid much board to my parents. I was a mooch! On payday I'd be out spending all my money on booze and more booze. That's all I wanted and girls of course!

I met one soon after the army. She was my age and from the next town. We'd already known each other from school years before. She said a bunch from her town and some from another town were going over to Staten Island for the day, and that I should go too. I met her over there. I took her to a restroom somewhere not very nearby, and when we got back, there was a fight going on with some New York guys. One of our gang got stabbed and we all hung outside the hospital for quite a while hoping he wouldn't die. He did, OK.

After taking her home that night in my buddy's car, we were off to a love affair that would land in pure hell, except for two beautiful children. We stayed together for about three years. We hated each other. I'd go out for cigarettes and come back three days later. I never came home on paydays, all the while getting locked up for different types of disorderly persons' charges; once all the way to the grand jury on a narcotics charge even though I was innocent. We proved it and I was found not guilty. Thank you very much!

I always drank till the lights went out. No matter where I started out, coming out of a blackout I could never remember how I got somewhere. I'd get my bearings, try to shake it off a little, and steal a car to get home. I would just park it up the street somewhere. I don't know how many times I did that. I do know what made me pay attention. I got caught eluding arrest about five motor vehicle charges. It was grand theft auto, assault on a police officer, willful and wanton disregard of the personal safety of others, and escapes. I'd make it through the roadblock and another forty-five minutes before they caught me. While being handcuffed behind my back in the police car, I got maced up close.

Within six days in the county, I got bail money from a New York "loan agent" with the help of a friend and his connections. I was an iron worker at the time at the World trade Center and the Meryl Lynch Building. I paid off the shark in installments, was off to more drinking, and got fired.

A friend of a friend had some carnival games and needed help. Thought I'd try that for a while and I loved it. It fit my needs perfectly— travel, daily cash, and women in every town. Once the mother of my two children hunted me down and I went home for a while. I was not content. My kids were great but she and I were enemies. It couldn't have worked! I did many disappearing acts, more booze, and more arrests. She'd had enough and so had I. Back to Mom and Dad's for a while, or back to the show. Then I had to come back to answer for charges and the judge said, "Indefinite three years." That meant how many months you'd get from the classification committee at the jail. I should have done maybe eight and a half months, but because of bad behavior, I did thirteen months. It was 1972 then, and I ran into a good friend and her new man. Holy Moly! What a party! They left for California after we partied for a month. My parole officer said I couldn't go. So, I was back to the midway and glad to be with the show again. I knew almost every carnie there, but there were always new ones (one day a chicken, next day feathers). We just kept moving and I liked it!

Carnival

OK, carnival life is much different, but it will always be a way of life only a few will know. A road less traveled, the carnival life was hard work. At the same time it was a family many had nowhere else. There was the competitive side, and there was the comradery. When there was trouble, we would always help each other out. There were breakdowns on the road, breakdowns of games, and even borrowing stock to get through the night.

We would see the same people in good times and bad. How they acted in adversity, whether they were strong or needed help with certain things, and basically know their methods so you'd know how to beat them in certain situations while competing for the mark's money. This could be open early or late, bigger prizes, locations, easier wins, etc. The townies only had what they had in their pockets and it was up to us to get it. We'd do whatever it took to get them to play our games before they played elsewhere.

When I first started, I ran some games that were called alibis. You could only win if I let you, that would be when I thought you had spent enough money and then you'd get a small prize. That was only to make you think that the game could be beat, I didn't like the cheating, nor was I enjoying the money I won/stole. I didn't run that joint for the whole week!

From there I went to what is called a hanky-pank. This could be a duck pond or any game with a winner every time. All these would require a truckload of teddy bears to keep restocking the shelves. People would see others walking away with prizes and know they could win too. There were a lot more smiles on their faces and I enjoyed that much more. What we were actually doing boiled down to selling teddy bears. If you played enough you would win. Some games required skill, so play and learn enough and you might still win. There were some that were just very hard to master.

My Game

I ran one such game for most of my career on the midway. In that game was a bottle lying down and you were given a stick with a string holding a curtain ring. If you are able to place the bottle in an upright position, you'd win a choice of the stand and all big stuff. It was very hard to do but I was always out there making it look easy. If you can't show a game like that, people won't play! Some were even amazed at how easily it could be done. They didn't know how long it took me to get that proficiency.

It was a lot of work running games. After, you'd tear them down, load them on a truck, drive to the next spot, and set them up again. Only once can I remember when there was no break in between shows. There was just enough time to get there, set up, and open for business. I was a much younger man then and managed when I wasn't drunk. I'd go MIA (get drunk) on tear-down night and drink during breaks, not during show hours. It was our way of life and I loved it!

In the next town, the jumps were a real treat because I always drank then. My problem was not having a good driver's license so I had some mild coronaries on some of the trips. There were weigh stations and any cop in sight was a danger for me.

At night, after the show closed, I got drunk as I could. The late starts were exactly what I needed to recoup for another of the same.

Some fairs called "still dates" were just somewhere to be while waiting for the next moneymaker. We didn't always have a state or county fair, so we were just looking to make expenses for the week. Every bit of it was always a gamble; one day chicken, next day feathers! When we won big, we'd spend big. Even good spots could get rained out or a bad wind could blow you over, so there were no guarantees.

Most of the time I lived in motels but during hard times, it was the back of the truck. That wasn't all that bad after you've had some practice with it. I had a big empty truck with electric and necessities. Some fairgrounds would have showers and sometimes it was in between north and south on RT #1 in Perrine, Florida with a hose hanging on a truck mirror.

Much of life happens while we are making other plans like all the preparation for the Great Pocono State Fair! It was at the race track while the track was closed. Like all other fairs, there would be entertainment. When we heard who it was, we all knew it would attract a big crowd. What nobody could predict was the brutal heat wave going on right then. We had all caught up on necessary repair to our games and equipment and spent most of what we had doing it. It was a much anticipated spot because it was a first.

This was in 1972 and these entertainers were at the top of their game. They were to include Bob Hope, Sammy Davis Jr., Helen Reddy, Mac Davis, the Jackson Five, and more maybe. The first night, we heard Bob Hope was paid $25,000 for his appearance and they sold $2,500 in tickets. That's a bad sign but not our problem. Our problem was that the exit let the small crowd straight into the parking lot and that's where they went. They got in their cars and there we sat! That was a bad deal there!

The show made them change the exit or we would have pulled stakes. They did, but all those people just walked on through like it was a freaking parade. I did manage to snag a few but it was like pulling teeth. It went this way for the week!

A show might have a G-top. That is where there is gambling at night. This time a guy showed up at Pocono with a converted tractor trailer. It was a snack bar serving hamburgers and beers and whatever, and in the back was a TV room that he let his son handle. Typically sharp carnie kid, he would charge 10 cents to sit down and a nickel to get up if they had to use the restroom it would cost. If they wanted a hamburger, it would cost extra and the kid would go get it for them. That kid did pretty well from what I saw.

At night the stand-up snack table would get flipped over and it was a beautiful crap table (a big dice pit is what it is). I was there every night and although I did win some money, I never left until they had all of mine. At the end of the spot, I had to borrow money to pay my motel bill.

The only enjoyment I got from that whole spot was the KFC chicken joint on the independent midway. We all had to really hustle to make a few bucks and they couldn't cook chicken fast enough. They had this huge helium balloon with their logo on it and I'd shoot some bullets into it every night. In the morning, it was lying on the ground and every night it was back up. I shot it down almost every night we were there.

On our way to Ottawa, Canada, one of our trucks broke down. It was empty but we needed it for the Canadian stock that was cheaper than paying a duty on what we'd bring in. I was elected to fly back to the international dealer the next day after working all day. There were no big airports near this place so he chartered a small plane to get me there. I got some sleep before we got to Syracuse, New York to clear customs. Then back in the air for another hour to get where we were going. I was not very comfortable because it was getting dark and it had began to rain. That plane was not equipped for an instrument landing. I didn't think, but I tried to go back to sleep anyway. In no more than thirty minutes, he tells me to keep looking for blinking red lights.

I yawned and asked, "What? The airport?"

"No," he says, "mountains and light towers!"

After that you couldn't close my eyes with a vise. Finally we were descending, I could barely see a light and he says "I hope this is . . . (whatever the name of the place was)" I asked him if he was kidding me and he retorted that he'd not been there before. I promptly told him that I didn't care if it was Japan. I was not getting back in that plane. It was a scary flight for sure! This was a dead airport with one 40-watt bulb maybe. The only change I had was Canadian so I couldn't use the phone to call a cab. Finally I found a small office on the other side and got a cab to a motel right next to where the truck was being fixed. The next morning, I paid for the repair and was on the road by noon.

Back in Ottawa, there was more work to get my game ready for our best spot and I opened that day exhausted. We were busy from 9 a.m. right up until midnight every day for two weeks. The money was great!

We all needed permits to work in Canada, but we had a hassle on the way back into the United States because there were Canadians who would jump on and I guess they thought they needed to know who was leaving them.

After Ottawa, we could all appreciate a spot like a week in Reading, Pennsylvania. That wouldn't be so busy. I am sure every one of us needed a rest!

Most of the carnival days were good. There was much fun in what we were doing, but there were also problems and some trouble. We all learned how to adjust to almost any situation. To put a show like that on the road and then put it back together took some routine and some simple common sense. It also took an occasional impromptu invention; things would break and had to be fixed immediately even if we didn't have a replacement. There would be wire, tape, clamps, or whatever it took to get through the night. We'd have a proper fix on the way but kept our stuff running. When you shoot a water gun into a clown's mouth to be the first to break a balloon, you don't see two water pumps and an air compressor. There's a water tank, hoses, and a lot of electric. These trailer games don't look so good sometimes after a jump and it takes time to get them fixed for call time. That is the time you open your game's awnings. Maybe there is no one on the midway but that's what time the show wants everyone to make it look like a show.

There were people on the show that were on the run or hiding from something or someone. They are not all on the same show of course, but a show is a good place to hide. Some people are there forever. There is nothing else for them. There are kids growing up on the midway who can't read or write, but with chores and how to get money out of your pocket, they do excel! Seeing the same people every day was not always so simple. You may eat with someone one day and argue with them on another. When it was all over, we were still family. There were a few fistfights with town marks but only one with another carnie.

On the jumps, I was required to drive a truck but I didn't have a driver's license. I always rode with someone when we went to the diner after the show closed. Many nights we went to the motel to count and cut money. Then we'd play a game of dirty hearts to see who would go get us something to eat.

One of the benefits of being on the show was that I didn't get into much trouble with the law. Much of my drinking was done within walking distance or I would ride with another boozer although there were a few times when the drunk was crazy.

Macon, Georgia was a great spot to make money. It is, make as much money as you could and then drink as much as time allowed. With our pockets a bit more healthy, we were headed for Charleston, South Carolina. That wasn't such a good moneymaker but one helluva party town! There were a few days off before the first day of the fair, so we always got a motel and hit the bars. Even at 3 a.m., a cabbie would take you to a bootlegger for a bottle. That town was wide open!

We'd heard about a club that was always mobbed with women, so on a weekend night, I went there with some carnie (I don't remember who it was). It was so crowded I couldn't find him when I wanted to leave. His car was nowhere to be found in that massive parking lot, so I "found" someone else's car. I was so drunk I just drove it to my motel and parked it a few doors down. I think it was still there when we left a few days later.

Most of the girls coming up the midway wanted a stuffed animal and I had a truckload of them. Teddy bear or no teddy bear, I always had a new girl every week. There never was a spot that I didn't have a girl! Everybody on the show knew me as the guy who gets the girls. Sometimes, even a year later, the same girl would come looking for me. I told this one girl to come to my motel thinking the other one wasn't coming. She knew the other girl and drove on. That is just a shame because I would rather have been with her.

The guy I worked for was also my good friend. We screwed each other often but it was a game. There were never any hard feelings until something happened in Charleston. I don't remember it being a big deal but I was ready to leave the show and that's when I did. I was out of money and he knew it. That's why he thought I'd go to Florida with them. The only alternative for me and my girl was to find a job there without money or any transportation. I had too much pride to let him know I needed him, so the third time he sent someone to my motel to tell me they were pulling out, I just told him to say good-bye for me. The next day, I and my girl hitched a ride up to Jersey. We broke up soon after.

That was my last time on the show. I missed it for a while and would occasionally think about jumping back on but never did.

Let's move on to bigger and better things. Not that I'd stayed out of trouble on the road, but at home I couldn't go six months without getting locked up. Once, I was not guilty of stealing someone's key! I spent a night in jail, and paid a find (just one of many). Most of the time, I was guilty of disorderly conduct stuff. I was getting worse with the alcohol problem but couldn't see it myself. Everyone else easily could! I was having fun, except for the rough spots. Rough spots? Party hardy, get crazy drunk, and land in jail often. A small price we all paid. Not all of us, just the dumb ones.

Me and Charlie

It was February 1968 before my son was born, and living with his mother became unbearable. I thought I'd hitchhike to Florida with a buddy of mine that also wanted a break from married life. It was nineteen degrees, hitchhiking on the turnpike in the dark and half drunk seemed like a good idea at the time. Somewhere around Jacksonville, we got a ride from a guy that let us stay at his place. His roommate was a great guy too and when they went to work in the morning, we went looking for a job. No, we didn't! We went straight to the bars. Later when the two car salesmen got home, we all sat around and drank beer. We all did some different running around but drank first. All went well until we overstayed our welcome and my buddy fell asleep with a cigarette that burned a blanket from the guy's recently deceased mother. We were politely asked to leave. They were good guys and needed an excuse maybe. God bless both of them for their kindness, but being asked to leave was nothing new to either of us. There were no bad feelings but mine for my buddy, soon to get worse.

We hit Route 1 south from Fort Lauderdale and hitched a ride from a guy that left his wife in Chicago. He didn't have a clue as to where he was going either so we went to cruise along Collins Boulevard in Miami. Admiring the flash of the place, we went by slowly and I saw a girl walking and I hollered, "Hey dip shit (a nickname I'd given her years before)!"

She comes running over, kisses my cheek and asks, "What are you doing here?"

Her man was a good friend of mine and he was up at the coffee shop. We talked a bit. One couldn't help the other with any money, so we moved on. You can guess what his girl was doing!

Chicago had no plans and didn't mind if we rode around wherever with him. We spotted a carnival truck and followed it to the lot in Plant City. We messed around for a while where I beat a guy's game. Told him I didn't want the stuffed animal and how to run his bosses' game better. I didn't see anything I wanted to do there so I helped Chicago get a job and hit the road to north of Tampa somewhere. We met a guy that had a trailer in his big backyard that was pretty nice and that we could stay and work for him for about a week or so. Beautiful! We did that and hit the road again. We had both been on the phone for a couple of days and decided it was time to go home. We were somewhere on the water dead west of the Wicheewachee mermaid attraction and he gave us a ride out to the front of the place on to Route 19. In miles, we had to go about a hundred in the wrong direction to get back to Plant City where my really good buddy left his luggage in the trunk of Chicago's car. After two to three hours in the sun, we got picked up by this old hippie school bus. There was a man driving and a girl and her dog were sitting behind him. There were only three regular seats on each side and the rest were sleeping bags and luggage. I really didn't look back there so as to not intrude on their privacy. We hadn't gone a mile when the driver asked if we had any kind of drugs. I told him no but I had a bottle of Boones Farm Wild Mountain Grape. He declined so I sent the bottle to the back of the bus. The girl took it to the group so I looked back there. That's when I saw him on the floor. He was leaning against the emergency door with three or four people sitting Indian style facing him playing cards. He looked over someone's shoulder and we made eye contact. I immediately turned forward! I didn't want to be nosy but at the same time I felt on edge. The bottle came back and I took a big hit before putting it away. It was hot.

My partner had some rap going with the driver and his girl. They were going to the Keys to get some jobs and hang out for a while. The driver asked if we wanted to go with them. That was just about three weeks too late, so I told them we were headed north after we get my buddy's freaking luggage.

I was just watching the road looking for our turnoff when for some reason I decided to look in the back. It was only a second when I realized someone had moved over a bit allowing me to see that the guy facing me had no clothes on. In those few seconds, he looked at me with those burning eyes and I looked forward immediately. Now anticipating our turn it was another fifteen to twenty minutes before we got out. Thank you very much! Now we're headed east. He wasn't infamous yet but it was Charlie Manson. No we didn't swap ID's but I know it was him!

First Trip West

Now I was never a dummy. The difference was the alcohol. Just add alcohol and out comes an instant idiot! I thought I was hip, slick, and cool. I was an idiot at times. Lucky I had anyone to hang or party with because there were always problems of some sort. I was asked to leave a few places and was helped out of a few. "Shake the dust from my feet," I thought as I left those places and situations. The grass is greener somewhere else and that always was the case for me.

I've been called lucky at times but I think it was more like divine providence. Wherever I went, things fell into place; always a job, a girl, and a place to hang my hat. Then alcohol would get involved and the grass turned brown. There were a lot of people hurt and many burned bridges.

Moving right along, my friends came back to the east coast from California to visit and to pick me up to go back with them. They came on a bus with a thirteen-year-old girl my friend had been babysitting to pick up me and my girlfriend after buying a small van. We stopped at Lake McConaughy, Nebraska for five days of fishing and partying. We had rented a trailer complete with pots, pans, dishes, and silverware. It was a nice place.

We stopped in Vegas for a few drinks and moved on. But for that, the whole trip was drunk driving all the way coast to coast. My friend was really bad with throwing beer bottles out the driver's window without looking at the cars behind us. We all let him drive off by himself; he was so irrational. We couldn't stop him. After about an hour, he came back and let me drive. It amazed me how we never got stopped once. The van he bought from my father was legal in that respect, but the license plates he got jumping a fence at the junkyard. It was some six months later the van was sold with the bogus tags still on it.

Back Home Looking
at the Problem

*C*alifornia was cool but I only stayed about eight months, went to the beach and Orange County Jail three times for drinking violations. I had enough of that for a while and went back East. There I got a job, moving furniture. Moving furniture for a living is a tough job for anyone, but I liked it. When you do it long enough, you learn the tricks that make you faster and more efficient. It shows in the way you pad, pack, and carry, but mostly in that you don't damage household goods, walls, or floors. With sixty hour weeks, there was always some twenty hours of driving time. It was fun hitting the road, staying in shape, meeting people, making money, and spending it. It was all good until I realized I was spending all I made each day at the bar, and for the first time I wanted to do something about it. That was my first real hospital detox. There was one in 1969 but only to save a job that I lost after for the same reason anyway. After a few 24's (days without a drink), I started to realize something about end of my rope syndrome. Like it says in the big book of Alcoholics Anonymous, "there will come a time when there is no defense against the first drink."

That is when all you can do is "hold on to your ass like the rest of us, whips." This is a term I learned from a good friend many years later who now has over eighteen years of sobriety A tool in recovery is the Serenity Prayer. A few more are live and let live, easy does it, and more. Happy in my serenity and breezing through a day until something breaks all that and the insanity that may follow can be hardly dealt with. Then, no matter what, don't pick up on your addiction! How do you do this? While thoughts and emotions might be similar for all, the very trying times getting though this must be more difficult for some. Perception plays a factor in that. This experience can tell you how good it is, how simple it is, and at the same time it is not all that bad. A couple of cheap rationales thrown in and you're in trouble. Pretty much the first of any progress after you get through a bad situation is gaining strength for the next hectic moment, and they will come!

Don't drink no matter what means exactly that. If it means walking around in circles and barking at the moon, then you walk and bark! Tomorrow when you tell your friends you were barking at the moon it will be evident that you did whatever it took and you are still here.

Don't quit before the miracle! We learn these things and what happens to most of us? We go do the same thing expecting different results. Seven months after I got clean for the first time, I went back out there. This is insanity for sure!

A Look at Blackouts

*H*ave you ever heard of a blackout? Like many people addicted to alcohol, I was one of those blackout drinkers with eyes wide open and fully ambulatory, walking, talking, and having sex, yet unaware of any of it. Coming out of one of those is just like waking up. It's very strange coming too while doing something or being in a jail cell not knowing the charge. That is very scary! Then finding out how small the bail is and knowing that it is not a serious charge. I experienced that two days in a row. Both times were for drinking in public. One which was not so trivial is coming out of one of those blackouts driving a stolen car and running from the police. Another one after passing out at a party and waking up and finding $40 stolen from my pocket. I was also at my bar on a Wednesday night while thinking it was still Tuesday. Evidently, I had gone home and went back just as drunk as when I left. I came out of one blackout sitting on the edge of a bed in a motel on Harbor Boulevard right down the street from Disneyland with a needle in my arm and beaten up, not knowing the how and why of it. Occasionally, I had a fight for something I don't remember saying or doing. I have put myself in some dangerous positions often enough—trying to pick a fight with about eight guys but there were no takers (Thank you very much!), walking across a busy highway oblivious to the traffic, then crossing a busy set of railroad tracks blind drunk. Seeing this, you would think a person was retarded, but these actions happen without that person's awareness of any of it. People would see these actions and form an opinion of me.

That is what they saw and that is the person I am, or so they think. What else would a person think? A blacked out person is so deliberate no one would think he doesn't know what he is doing.

Gambling started with a $25 bet on a football game. That went good for a while. The bets got bigger with time and by the time the bets were for Super Bowl, it was $500. That was the closest one ever, right down to the last play. The family and gang all thought it was $50. And if I'd lost, I wouldn't have told them. After that was basketball. I never liked it but with a bet, you watch some. That was a bore until about after six weeks when I was down some $3000. That was a bad run and I was so mad for letting that happen. I moved to Las Vegas, Nevada. Even before that, I had been to a Gamblers Anonymous meeting and saw firsthand how sick we all got from the compulsion. That made me ease up a bit (not).

Could it be that the hatred that grew inside me every day of my life is what poisoned my mind? Over the years, there were many problems and many jail times. It was many years after I lost my family that the depression came. Even when all was well, it was impossible to understand. About seventeen years of depression which time I did a lot of writing out of boredom and frustration and it was the only way I had to vent. On and off with the alcohol, but it was at the beginning of those seventeen years that I was able to forgive my father for the way he treated me. Then the hate melted off. The depression was worse in the morning so that is when I wrote mostly for the escape value of it.

My girl got sick and I took care of her for three years. Before she died, I was already a broken man so I took it as good as I could. There is no clear explanation for it, but soon after that was the end of those seventeen years and it seemed to be my new beginning. I was for a while fully expecting the depression to come back and it never did. Without the alcohol, hatred, and depression, the anger, which always came with them, was also gone. Whoever I had become was gone forever. I am now so sure of this I can blame something the hatred did to me.

Some alcoholics, like me, are blackout drinkers. That is when you are full ambulatory but are not aware of any of it. This is especially difficult to recognize if you have a routine. You may think you remember driving home last night just because you've done it so many times.

In my case, this happened so many times that it was made light of. Did I wonder if I had a good time? Not at all because my "friends" told me that we had a blast. I thought that was funny back then.

Precisely, a blackout is a powerful and mysterious force. It is not triggered by a certain amount of alcohol so it happens at different levels of intoxication. When it starts, it cannot even be detected in a crowd.

My own blackouts have caused me to become aggressively amorous, ignorant, rude, disgustingly vulgar, criminal, dangerously violent, and insane. During a blackout, anything can happen. I knew all this but would not stop drinking.

I was with this woman on a Tuesday morning when she told me what we had been doing since that Sunday. I hadn't had a drink in about six months and decided to have a couple late that Saturday night. Then Sunday morning, I rode my mountain bike to the next town that was open early and got loaded fast. She told me months before that if I ever started drinking again, I was to call her so I did and she came to get me. I think I just left the bike. I blacked out right after she picked me up, then it was Tuesday and she was telling me that we had a good time. I missed it! There was never any recollection.

There was waking up at three in the morning in a jail cell, not knowing what I had done to get there. Of course that was scary, but after bailing out the next morning and heading straight to a bar, I blacked out again and woke up in the same cell the next morning.

When I lived in Las Vegas, I went to a bar with some coworkers after work. That bar was nowhere near where I lived but near my favorite casino, Binion's Horseshoe.

I had no transportation but that never mattered much. I was miles from home but would hitchhike home later. I drank and won more drinks on the pool table before I left. A half block from the Horseshoe, I blacked out. All I remembered was having $29 in my pocket when I left the bar.

That was around 7 p.m. The next awareness I had was waking up at 6 a.m. next to my beautiful girlfriend, with my side of the bed wet. She was a barmaid and came in late so I missed her often. When I saw her, I would give her some of the cash I worked for. She let on that we talked when she came in and having no recollection, I thought I'd take a chance. You see, I checked my pocket and there was a twenty dollar bill. I never left a casino with twenty in my pocket and could not understand how it happened.

"How much money did I give you last night?" I asked her casually, fully expecting her to call me some kind of bum.

She said, "a hundred dollars." I guess I did well at the Horseshoe and took a cab home.

During another blackout in Vegas, I went back to the bar where I had been in the night before to ask what I may have done. I talked to a pit boss I knew and he told me he saw me fall down into the table under a slot machine, cutting my eye wide open. The casino was prepared to take care of me but the two girls I was with told them they'd look after me. I woke with my pockets empty and I knew the girls did it. I knew their men and threatened them to get my money back.

There was a blackout at a party in California where I was told I just dropped to the floor while dancing. They put me on a pile of clothes on the floor in a bedroom, and I woke early to find two twenties missing from my pocket.

Another time was when I didn't remember leaving the bar to go to sleep in my car. I woke up with my wallet on the ground beside the car and my money gone. There were some people who saw some kids rob me and did nothing.

One time when I came out of a blackout, I was in a janitor's closet in a grammar school on a Sunday morning. I had no idea how I got there or what I may have done.

It was at the last minute when a nice girl invited me to a big New Year's bash with most of her family. I made a fool of myself and blacked out. The next recollection was at 6 a.m., sitting in a chair at her sister's house and everyone was still dancing. After casting many dirty looks my way, her father drove me home still drunk.

After a carnival closed one night, I went to a bar and blacked out rather quickly. I had no idea after of course but I woke with the worst black eye I ever had. Someone didn't appreciate something I did.

Gambling at the Showboat one night, I just got up and walked away leaving $390 on the blackjack table. The guy I was with came to tell me about it; they wouldn't give him my money because they knew he would rob me. I went back and got my money but blacked right out again.

Then there was this old man, a painter and buddy of mine, who was in a nursing home for rehabilitation from a mild stroke. I blacked out but vaguely remember throwing my car keys in the woods before I went in there. My friend wanted to lie on his bed but in my blackout, I was on his bed and the staff couldn't wake me so they called the police. I was arrested for drinking in public and brought to the county jail. My first awareness in any of it was when I heard the clank of steel doors and keys echoing off the cinder blocks, a very familiar sound. I knew I was in jail but where and why, I didn't know. With that sound was a guard saying, "You about ready to get out of here?" I didn't know anything but of course I had a "hell yeah" for the guy. When I hit the street was when I realized where I was and started walking to find a bar or a liquor store. I was getting sick and needed some alcohol but there was nothing in sight after about a mile of walking. I walked into a bank and told a lady I was out walking when I got sick and would she call me a cab. Just fortunate to have some money in my account, I had the cab take me to an ATM and straight to a liquor store before taking me home. I got the car two days later. There was a time when my driver's license was suspended for a drunk driving arrest. My vehicle was parked but I took it out during a blackout. I don't remember driving but I do remember talking to an alcohol counselor in the parking lot of the detox center and the twenty-eight-day program I had been through. I was still in my driver's seat asking her if I could get in, and as they had a waiting list, she said, "No," and I drove off blacking out again. I just have a blurred split-second memory of hitting something hard and bouncing off to the right. I was still blacked out in the living room floor when I woke to loud knocks on the front door. It was a police officer immediately telling his partner, "He's here," which immediately told me I wouldn't be for long. He asked me if I had a drinking problem as I was getting cuffed. Then he walked me past my truck and I saw the front left was wrecked. This blackout got me another D.U. leaving the scene of an accident, hit and run, no insurance, and driving without a license while suspended.

There was a blackout where I woke up in bed with two girls I knew. It was a strange place. I couldn't find the bathroom at first. Now aware, I had a plan but they were sound asleep so I went back to sleep. That had to be one of the times I couldn't be wakened because I woke later and they had left for work. Damn if I missed another one. I got up and left bewildered as usual.

In the U.S. Army I came out of a blackout getting hollered at as I was peeing on this sergeant's stereo. I was so loaded I could hardly move so he threw me across the hall. He just let me go back to my bunk, and it was never mentioned again.

There was one in Staten Island, New York at a bar called the Christmas Tree. It was a loud and crowded bar. I knew a few people that night, but this one girl kept coming up to me telling me that we had been together recently. I had no recollection and told her it couldn't have been me. She wouldn't take no for an answer, so we walked across the street to the woods to lie down on the weeds. I immediately blacked out and missed another one. I woke at daybreak and noticed we were on a bunch of poison ivy. This bar was in a wooden area and early Sunday morning there was no one around, but one lone car with a tag from my state on it. I looked in and saw a guy sleeping so I woke him up to ask for a ride for me and the girl. He agreed and we were off to find some booze somewhere. When we got to her home, she invited us in. Her huge boyfriend was passed out on the living room floor. I went to her room to discuss while my buddy kept an eye on big man. Then he went in to discuss. We were all still drunk. We had another drink and left. I and that guy spent the rest of the day in a bar.

There was that time I was staying at a crash pad most of the time. This is a place to go after the bar closes to continue to party or just find a spot to sleep. There was one full bed and a couch. The rest slept on the floor. One night I went in all by myself to find two girls in the bed. They said someone told them they could stay there. I said, "Sure, but this is my bed so move over." I jumped in next to this girl with black hair and blacked out. We had sex in the dark at some time and later, I looked out into the living room to see black hair on the couch. I had sex with the other one. We parted company in the morning; I never got a name.

One that we will never know is a blackout that happened an hour away from my sister's house where I was staying. Somehow I made it to their neighborhood and with a mile to go, I come out of it speeding on a gravel road with a stop sign very near. Instantly panicking, I locked up the brakes and skidded thru the stop street to the other side of the road before coming to a stop without hitting anything. I looked to my left to see a cop rolling up on me. I gave him a story about black guys chasing me and me going to my sister's house up the street. I mentioned the name because my brother-in-law was a fireman. I think that was what saved me that time. I don't remember getting to my sister's house but I was told that they took my keys and also parked a car behind mine in case I got up in the night. In the morning, I looked to see if my car made it home and thought I'd gotten away with another one. I drank some coffee and was heading out to do it again when I noticed blood splattered over the front of my car and what looked like a big bullet hole. Now that was a good scare. I listened for news about my last sixty miles but never heard any.

One bar I went to for a while there were always girls there and more on other nights. One night I noticed a good-looking girl looking at me more than once before she sent me a drink. That was very nice, thank you very much! We talked a bit before she asked me if I remembered what I'd said to her the night before. I didn't remember her from last night and she wouldn't tell me what I said. Of course I pumped her until she told me. She said my exact words were, "Why don't you put that set where it will mean something?" That was while admiring her endowment. She convinced me that I did say that before telling me we should go to another bar. I had about $10 in my pocket on our way to the lounge at the Holiday Inn where she knew the barmaid and got me a full glass of whiskey. We had a few of those and a few dances before she told me she already had a room. There was room service for more drinks. We had some food in the morning and then went off to a bar for a few. After about an hour, she drove me home and gave me $20.00 because she knew I was unemployed. She was nice but I never saw her again nor could I even remember our first encounter

These blackouts are nothing less than phenomenal! They cannot be predicted by anyone of the many people who are blackout drinkers. You don't know when the lights went out, you just know they did. You may wake up in your own bed but you don't know how you got there. There can be a hundred people intensely watching me drink and no one could tell when it started or when I came out of it.

The last one was about ten years ago where I live now. I thought I was fine at a 0.24 blood alcohol level and only got arrested because I was speeding. I had left my apartment area because the pay phone was not in a private area and I wanted to talk to my mom on the phone in a quiet place. On the way back, I didn't see this cop or I'd have slowed down. I pulled over and then I blacked out. I was in jail for two days before I came out of it. I called that my last one. Today, I am sure it was.

About Journaling

One night on TV, a man was talking about his time while writing, and it was very depressing. Then I remembered hearing the same about Stephen King. It must be common in many people who write. Most of my own writing was done while I was in some terrible moods. I have not been so in quite a while now and have just realized that I haven't written anything in about ten months.

It has been ten months since that depression left me, and this is the longest amount of time that it has been absent. Why now? People have told me I've done all the right things this past year. That, in itself, speaks volumes because this is my first good year!

Most of any progress I have made in the last year was due to God's plan and the 12-step group that I belonged to. Without either of those, I was always a loser. I put such importance on the wrong things, and never where it should have been, doing the things I should have been doing.

"I was fine, but I got over it" may be the mood of the day, but that is just one day. Tomorrow is another day and it isn't that far off. Of course that too shall pass, but if it doesn't, then maybe you need a doctor

A depression that sends you to a doctor is said to be treatable but there is no magic pill (at least there wasn't in my own recovery). The doctor sends you to the pharmacy, then it's back to the safety of isolation. There you sit and the writing begins. For whatever reason, much of it gets trashed. Nonetheless, the depression seems to be the creative factor for the most part!

Most of my writing are perceptions and recollections that seem to be outlining more of how bad it was and can be, rather than how much better it is now. When I realize how I perceive something differently is when I see my own growth.

There is not much direction in my life as far as any goal or anything else. I am not very involved right now, nor have I ever been. I am standing still right now, but I have hope that had previously been lost.

See Who I Am

Running the streets of Anaheim, Manhattan and places in between, many situations presented a challenge. Whether it was some work to get booze money, or some other way to get money that was legal or not, there was a sense of accomplishment, even over something trivial that went well because things usually didn't! This was only a two-minute satisfaction before another escapade. With each, a sense of victory over an obstacle I probably put in my own path. Stealing, conning and cheating in most cases, I really enjoyed all I got for free. Of course those freebies had a price I was yet to pay. At the time, I did not realize that I was paying with my life on a daily basis. When it is all over, there isn't much life left. Sometimes it results in an incapacitating depression with heavy remorse, regrets, and sorrow. Nothing was free at all.

One big thing I have going for me right now is that I can get by with little. I always have! The people I know who slave for the dollar are the people who must have things to make them happy; without those, they are not. I feel as though I am already spent. I had nothing to worry about, and I just try to enjoy whatever life I have left. This is only what we all want.

Now much older and a bit wiser in my decision making, I am not looking for all the excitement I can find. For years and years, I could never stay home at night. What if I missed something? What if something happened at the bar and I wasn't there? I remember at least one rare occasion I did stay home and it didn't feel right. Maybe they were wondering where I was? Did something happen to me? Why wasn't I at the bar? This is the kind of thinking that had me excited to go the next night. I would be back! I missed my friends (excuse me, this is where two positives make a negative). Yeah! Right! My friends? That was only what I thought in my very limited capacity. None of these people were my friends. If they are just drinking friends, then they are just that! Nobody wondered where I was that night. Nobody even knew I wasn't there. Just like me on any other night, the pool games went on, the darts flew and the drinks went down. Where Bill or Bob is didn't cross my mind. It was just another night chasing the buzz and the girls. If a regular wasn't there, did I think of where he may be? Hell no! He took a night off or whatever. I could care less. I never thought about any of that, but I went on thinking I'd be missed if I wasn't there. This is ludicrous when you see it from afar. Not at the time. The thinking is not always according to logic. It is the perceived logic of the day, believing only in myself and never even thinking I could be wrong. Italian Pete called me *gabadone*, which translates to hard head. Mexican Bob called me *torpe* (spelling), a word meaning stubborn. This is simply an attitude that will never learn anything, an unyielding resoluteness that will not be deterred—total blind ambition.

Whatever you call it, it does not contribute to harmony. Whether among coworkers or in a social group, nobody likes a know-it-all, but when you are that person, you don't see that.

Much time goes by and you finally learn from your mistakes. You lost a lot of time because you didn't know what you needed to know. The fact that you now know what you should have known then only lets you know how wrong you were.

Has my logic always been faulty? Will I ever learn? I can still look back at some recent days when I had it all together and realize. "No, I didn't." This just alerts me to examine my decisions more thoroughly. It must only be that I'm a slow learner.

One Opinion

Although there were many drugs on my plate, my choice was alcohol. This is what I refer to when talking about addiction, compulsion, temptation, and recovery.

After detoxing, there are many temptations that come, even in such an innocent form as suggestion. Any one of these can bring agreement with this "good idea." Whatever it is in addiction, the power of suggestion is great! Even when no longer active in addiction, the power of suggestion would still be many but may have no power over the addict because the appeal is gone. To an addict, this is tantamount! This is a miracle. The way I see it, it is a way to win my life back. I believe that only divine intervention could have relieved the compulsion to self-destruct.

Because sobriety is new to us, those like me would still not be of the right thinking for an indefinite perod of time. Then, when coming from the bottom of despair, depression, futility, remorse, etc., you will begin the process of building a better life. Now you have problems you didn't have before because until now you never tried to fix anything. The problems would mount and penalties would be paid, but rectifying the situation was impossible then.

One at a time we can eliminate these things. It is now possible to repair some of our past. Everyone has problems, but not everyone has trouble. All I ever had was trouble! Now we are making some progress.

To be successful, this must be done slowly. At times we will make some good progress that just might happen without much effort on your part. More often it will be baby steps, but that is still good progress. You cannot make things happen if the time isn't right. You will learn easy does it and find comfort in any progress no matter how small or insignificant it may seem at the time. The carnage from our old life will eventually disappear and allow a new sense of freedom we never knew before (If you've ever been in jail and got out? It's something like that).

Today my faith is helping me win my life back, as well as my self-respect and the respect of others. This is helping me smile, all the while never letting me forget how I cried. Sure I cried but I never really did anything to relieve the misery.

When the mind-set has changed, the suggestions steadily lose their influence. As we get stronger, they just tend to remind us how weak we once were. Today, I am strong. Therefore suggestions are weak and ineffective. I win a new life simply by changing my mind. How simple is that? But is there another day?

There is so much help for a troubled mind in some of the self-help books that are recommended for reading. Some of these that I found most helpful were written by Dr. Norman Vincent Peale. One in particular is *The Power of Positive Thinking*. He was a great man of God who had a true concern for humanity. Another help for me was *Erroneous Zones* by Wayne Dyer. This is a book I would recommend to anyone and everyone, even if you don't make errors in your life. Many great books were written by Robert Schuller, pastor of the Crystal Cathedral in Garden Grove, California. These focus on possibility thinking which is absolutely necessary in recovery!

Many self-help books can be beneficial. It just takes being ready for any of it to be realized. If you are not ready, it just seems like a good idea for other people. You may need to read a book a second time before any of it will be absorbed. Then, more and more is understood and there is even excitement in the process.

You may have heard "If you forget the past you are destined to return to it." This holds true with addiction but the further you are from it, the more it loses its power over you.

Most of it is mind-set. I am now totally removed from the misery I once lived in, created by the assumption that it always had to be that way. Therefore, I did nothing about it.

I truly believe that God will help those that help themselves. That gives me some of his power as long as I am seeking his will for me.

This is so much easier to win than the constant struggle I was in all alone!

Score Somewhere

There is no serenity in excitement and travel because you need to always be on your toes. On the way, you will take care of necessities like housing and food, all the while satisfying the habit. The traveling addict will always find the liquor store and/or a place to score drugs. Anytown, United States has a neighborhood where drugs are sold. You will surely be alert going into these situations. I have been to some backstreets in Boston, abandoned buildings on Staten Island, alleyways in downtown Baltimore, and on some runs that were sixty to seventy miles round-trip just to score.

One such adventure was in Tennessee just after renting a house trailer near Oak Ridge National Laboratory where I eventually got a job (with a Q cleared escort of course). Soon after we got settled, it was time to go find some marijuana.

We drove down to Knoxville to find the projects where there were always drugs. Turning on to that street, I saw a black-and-white police car going around the other corner very slowly. I slid up on some guys and copped a bag just as the cops were coming back around behind us. They didn't see me, so we just drove off. About two miles up the street in a 7-Eleven parking lot, I am cleaning some weed on my road map, and without looking up, I see a car rolling up on us. Very casually, I slid the weed back into the bag and looked up as if surprised to see them. This car had a driver with three more cops in it. They were so obvious they had to think everyone was a dummy not to know who they were. The driver was close enough to reach out and shake my hand. Then he asked me if I was interested in a truck driving job. I suspected that he wanted my name and address. Holding up my map, I declined and asked for directions to somewhere; I had out-of-state tags and I guess I looked like a tourist? They drove off and we went up the road to roll a joint for the ride back to our trailer. It was the same thing in Albuquerque, Denver, and everywhere else we went. It was not so easy every time, but we were always able to do it!

He Didn't Like Me,
I Hated Him

At one time after four to five years of silence, my son called me. We had a long talk and he said he'd call me the week after that, that was twenty months ago. Ask me if I am surprised. Only through the grapevine did I hear he was at his mother's. Of course, I couldn't call him there. He said that even after thirty years, if she knew he was talking to me, she would have a fit. There is some hatred going on there. I know something about hate because as I recall, I hated my own father every day of my life until I was forty years old. He never talked to me. He never taught me anything; he never had a minute for me. He wouldn't help me when I asked. One time while trying to stay sober, I was leaning over tying my bootlace, when he came around the counter to pour a shot of whiskey right in front of my face and left the bottle sitting there. I walked away before he came back to drink it. I didn't drink that day but there was another time he surely wanted me to fall.

My family knows the rough deal I got from my father, and although saddened by all the years we lost, today I love him as if I always did. Of course my mom saw the change and was happy about it. I am happy about it too, no matter how long it took.

This is why I hope my kids forgive me, even if I never know it. Hate is like taking poison and waiting for the other person to die. I suppose this will only happen when my kids see the waste occupying their minds. It will be the same "load lifted" that I experienced some twenty years ago.

Some things never change. With my alcoholism in a rage, he probably changed long before I knew it. He saw me struggling to stay sober, and then the phone would ring with another bail request and we'd go ten steps backward. Left to my own resources, which were nil, I guess I went ten steps backward on my own.

It just ain't over till it's over. For today, thank God it is!

Inmate on Tour

New Jersey became a bore for me sometime around 1976, so I thought I'd go back to California for a while. I needed to get away from a gambling habit that was way out of control. There was a misunderstanding with the law before I left California the last time and I had two warrants out for my arrest on a charge of petty theft and assault. I didn't steal anything nor did I hit anyone but that was the deal. Regardless, I was hot. In Quartzite, Arizona, I switched license plates registered to an alias but didn't have a driver's license to go with it. The speed limit then was 55 mph and I was all alone in the desert cruising along at 85 mph and a California highway patrol appeared in my blind spot. He gave me two tickets after listening to a bunch of lies. I begged him not to give me a ticket, when that's all I wanted. I'd broke down in Phoenix the day before and got pretty wasted at a bar nearby, but my car started at 3 a.m. and I hit the highway with a little buzz. It was a few hours later with that cop so I was looking a little better. He was such a typical California highway patrol cop but he bought my "can't find my license" story.

A few hours later, I checked into a motel in Los Angeles and called my good friend, the sister of the mother of my two children. We were always good friends and of course, were accused of sleeping together but we never did. I kissed her once, and that's a fact!

Having moved out of Orange County, she was now living in Lom

Poc where there is a federal prison holding her man. Whatever day it was, it was the first of two days a week when there was no visiting allowed, so she said, "Where are ya? We'll be right down; call ya when we get there." It was about 200 miles for them to drive so I went out for a bottle and some cards for family and then took a nap. Pretty soon, the phone rang and she wanted directions to my room. In a minute, there was a lot of noise coming up the stairs and I gave her a big hug. Looking over her shoulder, I saw a bunch of girls coming up. She said, "Oh them? They are just some of my friends. Well do come in!" In a short while, we were off to a Samoan bar we used to hang out at in Santa Ana. There, we ran into a good friend from back East who we didn't know would be there.

Originally scheduled to meet an old girlfriend of mine, I called her and after a while took off to a motel. The next morning, I wanted to go back to the bar of course. To my surprise, all the girls were there and so was my other buddy. After many beers and pool games later, because it was a beer bar, I had to go to my car and fill a beer can with whiskey. My girl got mad because I didn't want to leave so she left. Oh well! I guess I'll try to deal with what's left. Are you kidding me? That place was full of girls. My friend always fixed me up with her girl friends, but this time she outdid herself. The only problem was that they were all prisoners' girls. They all lived in Lom Poc where I decided to go

We stared out for a 200-mile trip with a good alcohol buzz. We were not really drunk, but we had a good buzz going on! Way up in some mountains in Santa Barbara County on Highway 101, as usual I was sitting on 85 mph when I went around a turn and I saw a California highway patrol giving a guy a ticket. In two seconds we were around the bend of the mountain and out of his sight. I never thought he'd come after me, so I kept it on 85 mph! It must have been twenty to twenty-five minutes and there I was getting pulled over. One of the girls was nineteen years old and we had an infant with us. I quickly told her to put my half pint of whiskey under the wet diapers in the diaper bag. This guy was some bastard. He checked my registration and wasn't real happy about my lost driver's license story. The tags were from Alabama and I told him I was too. He didn't believe me for a minute! He then proceeded to put me through every field sobriety test he could think of, some of which I'm sure he had just made up. "How do I know you are who you say you are?" He persisted! Meanwhile all I kept up with was the fact that I'd just gotten a speeder down South by one of his compadres and requested for him to give me a break 'cause I had just moved to California and my license was going to be bad enough with the tickets I already had. The other one was for no license in possession also! He continued to be the biggest bad guy he could be and I continued with the "please, please, please don't give me a ticket act," when of course that is exactly what I wanted him to do. So, more please, please, please, and just to be a real bastard he gave me a speeding ticket and another "no license in possession" ticket. Now he felt real good about himself! You could just see it on his face the way he was so satisfied with ignoring my pleas. He had to be even more thorough and insisted on getting the address where I'd be in Lom Poc. What an ass that guy was. It freaked me out when a car pulled up behind us and he said I'd have to wait while he finished giving this other guy his ticket. Yeah! The guy he had when I passed him. It just made him so mad because I never even slowed down.

So, now in California about three to four days and even my alias was hot. I knew I had a little time in the area, so I had a lot of fun with the girls. I went to see my friend in the joint once but they wouldn't let me in because I was too drunk. So, I had some more fun with the girls. My alcoholism caused me a lot of trouble but that week was "Use your imagination and double it!"

In a day or so, a husband was getting out on furlough, also my freedom in jeopardy, I decided to call the other girl who was now in Fresno. Up there I just hung out trying to figure out what to do. I knew that sooner or later, I would be apprehended by the local constabulary so I said, "Let's go to Vegas." It was me, her, and three kids aged four, six, and nine in two vehicles. We got there on a rainy Friday night with $50. I changed my tags back and even had "sort of a driver's license" to match.

Las Vegas was a very interesting place, to say the least! Without any money to rent anywhere, we thought of camping at Lake Mead would be good for a while. It was twenty-five miles into town where some work was to be found. The next afternoon, I got a job driving rental cars from one location to another. It didn't pay much but I had five mouths to feed. Daily pay would take me to the store on the way back to the lake. My girl and the kids were looking for some food when I got back. It wasn't all that good but after ten days or so, we got a motel room on Boulder Highway, near the Showboat. Then there was payday, heavier drinking, and chaos soon after.

Soon there was the first of many lockups for being drunk in public. They called it protective custody. Mostly it was exactly that, as I was not capable. Then after six to eight hours or when they got tired of hearing me hollering, they kick me out. No court and no charges are filed.

In a trailer farther down Boulder Highway, there was gambling and drinking at one of four bars within a minute's walk. It didn't take very long to be barred from one of them. They'd let me have a couple of drinks but wanted me out. I didn't like the place anyway and I'm sure they knew that.

One thing my girl neglected to tell me was that the Volkswagen camper bus she was driving belonged to a friend who was just letting her use it. Apparently this guy was upset over services no longer provided, plus the fact that he's out a new vehicle, the bus was reported stolen. At 1:00 a.m. on a Saturday morning, they came banging on the trailer door. We had packed stuff for a hike with the kids in the morning and were asleep. I slammed the door open growling until I saw who it was and mellowed out real fast. They put her in their car immediately and started on me. I had lost the registration and the title to my car so I was charged with grand theft auto and some other fugitive made up stuff. After three days in the Clark County Jail again, they let me out with no charges filed. At the same time they let her out with no charges either. The guy wanted his camper back. The kids stayed with a neighbor until her parents came to take them back to California. They were gone before we got out of jail.

She and I became incompatible from then on. She moved out somewhere and had another man soon after. He was another drunk. Boy could she pick them! She was a nice girl. Go figure?

When I was in jail that time, there was a Mexican guy I knew from California and they let him out the same time as the both of us. She was leaving so I told him he could have the couch. I never knew it before but this guy liked to drink like I did. He's a dynamite guy but got crazy much faster than me and I had to babysit him a few times to keep him out of jail.

He liked to gamble as much as I did so one night we scraped together $5.00 to gamble with. The town of Henderson was closer than Fremont Street so we headed there. There was not enough money for two guys to sit and gamble so I let him do it. I let the cocktail girl know that half of it was my money. It will be scotch and water, Thank you very much! Time goes by and I'm just standing around watching all the girls and my friend is poking me to take a look at what he's doing. He now had fifteen $5.00 chips up for a bet and caught a blackjack on it; that pays one and a half times your bet. Beautiful indeed! I should have grabbed some but didn't and he gave it all back. Now we are drunk hitchhiking in the dark and some guy pulls up seeing how drunk my friend was he was going to pull away when my friend punched him in the face. He drove off in a hurry; we got a ride in a minute and made it back to our neighborhood.

I had been frequenting a bar nearby and really liked the barmaid. She knew it but that was as far as it went. I still lived across the highway and would be in her bar every day or night, letting her know in one way or another.

Another night on our way to gamble, Valdez and I stopped at her bar for a few before we went to the Showboat. After many drinks and all the money gone, it was time to hitch a ride back (This time period must be one of the three times my car was impounded). My friend was so drunk he was running around a lit up car lot looking for one with keys. I dragged him out of there two or three times before we got a ride and were home safe once again. I poured him into the trailer and went to see the barmaid. After telling her how poorly we did, she bought me a drink. The night was winding down and I was just doing my regular when she asked what I would be doing later.

I said, "I don't know. Why?"

Then she said, "'cause I am gonna take you home with me!"

Trying to be casual I said I'd be right back. I practically ran home to take a shower and was back over there for a few more drinks. If I wasn't a drunk, we most probably would have stayed together. She was a sweetheart from day one! Nonetheless, like everything else that was good in my life, I drank up the love that could have been.

Vegas is a haven for gamblers and drunks. I was both. It was never planned but I never stayed drunk for more than a month nor did I stay sober for more than a month. Gambling every day, I gave back most of whatever I won.

I spent almost two years in Vegas and ten times in Clark County Jail, mostly for drunk charges and being arrested for walking out of a snack bar without paying. There was a drunk driving charge that had been satisfied for over six months when some bounty hunters came to get me.

This lady came to my open door asking if I was the name on a piece of paper. I said, "Yes," and she motioned for her male partner who came in holding a gun. They were misinformed but had their job to do and I went down for two days without an apology again. That was the only time I had ever been sober in Clark County Jail.

Clark County Jail dormitories are a three-minute walk to the mess hall, passing a few big holding cells that were usually empty this time of the year. It was a cold area and one morning, there was a nude man on the floor with blood coming out from everywhere. He must have been unconscious or he would have known how cold he was. He was still there motionless on our way back. He was more than likely just an idiotic drunk who mouthed off to the cops. If you act like a tough guy, they gang up and beat you pretty bad. This is by no means unique to Vegas.

More drinking, more jail. Eventually I'd had enough! With no more girl, no more car, and somewhat depressed, I figured I'd go back to Jersey for a while. I think it was my sister again who got me a plane ticket. I was drunk when I left Vegas and got drunker that night when I got back East.

While visiting all those different jails, there would be guys with all sorts of charges. Sometimes they would come back from court and tell me what they got for their crime. With differing circumstances there can be no set punishment for a crime. Much of it depends on your priors! You can be pulled over for stealing a car and get grand theft auto! Or not pull over and the same crime turns into added charges like speeding; almost getting caught but getting away gets you an escape charge and running a roadblock and hurting a cop gets you more time for each offense. When you go to court having already made a deal with a plea bargain, they drop some and hang you forever if they want on that one charge. It's not fair but that's the way they do it. When I had to answer for that assault and petty theft deal in California, it was after three days in Orange County Jail that the public defender came in to tell me he got the charges lessened to some kind of disturbing the peace or something. I could plead guilty and be released with time served.

"Do you want to do that?" he asked,

I said "No, but that's what I'll do."

I did that to be released that afternoon. I wasn't guilty of anything but they wanted convictions and that's what they got. I saw some guys doing time just because a judge thought they knew something and wouldn't tell. They took the 5th and were jailed for contempt. To me that was just ludicrous. One of them was Little Nicky Scarfo and another I heard was called Frenchy. His name was something like Ladiere. I saw them coming through admissions and departures where I worked. Ladiere got wacked (killed) two to three years after they let him out. I figure he knew something.

Our judicial system is not science and it doesn't always work like it should, but this is the only system we have. For my first felony conviction, I got three years when I should have been given probation. My second one, also violent, should have gotten me time and I got three years' probation.

That part of me was long ago and I know it will never happen again!

No More Family

They were babies!

It still breaks my heart to think of how good it could have been to raise my own children. Of course they don't know that I've been praying for them every day for the last twenty years. I guess that was when I began to change some. Maybe? What they need is a mother who is always there for them, so I also pray for her.

Those kids were told lies about me, but me being an irresponsible drunk was true. I was never there to show them anything different. Some of what they heard about me were not lies but I don't know any of it for sure.

I believe in part that she was a good mom but will never understand why she would hurt her own children by putting me down . Wouldn't it hurt to hear about your dad being a bum? I was never there so they just had to believe that I was off somewhere being a bum.

Let's suppose that the mother had some skeletons in her own closet. Why would I ever want my kids to know these things? We could start with her cheating and end on the same note. That alone was reason enough to leave her and could at least explain part of my absence. It does not excuse a total desertion!

That woman had so much hate in her that she could not see beyond her own personal vendetta. Rather than protect them, she wounded them to hurt me. My kids don't have much use for me. She taught them well!

Regrets? I have a few!

When my son was eighteen, he told me, "I know now that you could never have stayed with her. You're just like me!" That pretty much explains why she favors her daughter. I saw how her parents favored her over her sister and how she favored one of her nieces over the other. There was no trying to hide it. It was always so obvious.

I knew for a fact that there were times when my kids wanted to get away from their mother so why fault me for doing exactly what they wanted to do?

Most dads probably have trouble telling their sons that they love them. (Mine was a different problem). It was with little difficulty when I told my son for the first time as an adult. He was eighteen and told me he'd never heard anything like that when he was growing up. So, looking at their mother and I, you might suppose that actions speak louder than words. Maybe they do, but the words count too! Just as my being missing in action was inexcusable, so was her "hell on wheels" style of love.

Some alcoholics can do a good job of being a father. As for me? I didn't have a clue! Not an excuse but I never had one to model myself after. One thing I am certain of is that had I stayed around, I'd have been loved by both of them.

I have one picture of my daughter only because my son gave it to me. I have some of him because I took them myself. They are included in my daily prayers when I mention family but I often say their names when I ask God to take care of them in my absence.

Insanity Prevails

New Jersey bars close at 2 a.m. and 3 a.m. on the weekends. Last call for alcohol? I don't think so! All drunk but not enough! Without a car of my own, I would just take someone else's and head over to New York to have a few more drinks, usually getting a six-pack and then hit the tunnel. I mean hit the tunnel!

Once on the turnpike, it was very foggy and I was about to pass out. I thought I'd get off and run along the lighted streets to keep me awake. It didn't help much because I was still nodding out. I turned on the radio, stuck my face out the window, and even slapped myself in the face a few times. Nothing worked! I was still ready to pass out with miles to go, so I just kept on driving. Well into a nod and doing about 55 mph on a three-lane highway, I opened my eyes to see a red light. One car stopped dead in each lane in front of me. I was in the middle lane and closing fast. It was instant panic that I felt! Jamming on the brake and turning sideways, I think I hit all three cars at the same time, lessening the impact. The car I was in stalled out and the drivers, I think, got out of their cars. All the stuff I did before to wake up didn't work but this did! Well, what have I got to lose? The car started back up and I took off down a side street. I knew all the roads and was able to elude a possible pursuit although doubting there was one. Parking the car up the street, I went home and went to sleep. I did escape any prosecution, but I did not escape the insanity that was building its home in my head.

I had another return trip from the city in a stolen car I left with its front end off the ground. You cannot see where you are going with your eyes closed. There was no other car in sight, so I ran up the road, stuck my thumb out, getting a ride from the first vehicle that came by. I got away with that one too, but for the "getting nuttier" part.

There are way too many of those to remember. Sometimes I would steal contents, one I ran over a cliff, and one got parked up the street for my use every night for about a week. I never had a driver's license!

When I started running carnival games, we did some Italian festivals in Manhattan and Brooklyn.

At one of those, the future mother of my two children was working a joint up from mine and enjoying all the attention she was getting from the New York boys. This of course had me upset so I got a break and went to the bar. She would be sure I saw what she was doing! She knew I loved her but kept it up. She cheated on me more then I'll ever know and that's a fact. After being back at the bar for the third time, I decided not to go back.

I called a cab and thought some beer for the ride to Jersey was a good idea and so did the cabbie. He even went in to get it and for some reason, I got out and walked off. We were only about four blocks from the Holland Tunnel so I stuck out my thumb and got a ride in about four minutes. It was well after midnight and these two guys were on their way home from seeing a band. They were telling me all about it but I just told them where to let me off and passed out. They woke me up just when they were about to cross a bridge into Pennsylvania; about forty miles from where I needed to be. Now I'm in some quiet little town miles from nowhere! The only thing I could do was to steal a car to get home. The first car started right up but it apparently had a bad clutch and I couldn't get it in gear. I was trying to jam it in reverse anyway making a hell of a noise. You could have heard that for miles; it was so quite there. I went to the very next car in this tiny complex and took off in that one. Still very drunk, I had a hard time keeping it on the road. I do remember some road construction barricades that only came into view because they were blinking. Then I heard a bang and saw one flying off to the right, but that was enough to keep me awake and to notice that the gas tank was on empty. I got some gas and made it to my parents' neighborhood. I parked up across the tracks, walked about five minutes, and went to sleep. I thought I was slick because I got away with another one. The insanity of it all cannot be measured!

Another Felony

It was quite a while since my girl and I moved out of our old place, where the landlord was attracted to her, but we moved and that was the end of that. We lived in different towns, but were reunited easily by the train. It was a busier town where she lived and she ran into this guy on the street. After he told her some lies about what he heard me say about her, she was real hurt and came to me crying. I hadn't said any of those things and let it go. I didn't forget! I'd been sober for about six months and although I really wanted to go after that guy, I didn't. Then one night I had a few drinks and getting him became my top priority. I lived on Broadway in this little town where people hung out on every corner. I looked out of my window and saw a guy I knew standing with his friend. In a minute, I asked my friend to ask his friend if he'd give me a ride across the bridge to go beat this guy up. First I banged on the door, then opened it up and walked in swinging a fist at him. I beat him all the way to the hallway and as he went down, I kicked him and thought that was enough. He went for the phone so I ripped it off the wall. I didn't even know my buddy was in the house behind me and he beat the guy in the face some more.

I was in a town where people knew me, but they didn't know where I was staying then. I just kept a low profile for a while. I knew they would hunt me down eventually, so I called a cop who I knew and asked him how bad it was. First he asked me where I was and I told him to *forget about it*. He said it was bad and that I should turn myself in. I didn't think that was such a good idea, so I made plans to leave the state.

Down in the Baltimore area I knew some people, so I just hung around there drinking for about three weeks. That was getting old and I missed my girl so I thought I'd go see what happens. Bad idea!

The bail was set at $10,000 without any 10 percent to a bondsman. They Wanted it all! Of course there was no way out, so I went to the county for a while. I didn't realize it at the time but I was so strung out on alcohol that the jail doctor put me in the hospital section to detox; I was sicker than I thought.

After the detox, I was put in what they call a special needs unit because I was still then somewhat crazy. Beautiful! This part of the lockup had every imaginable nutcase there was. There were a bunch of gays, rapists, those with similar charges that hadn't yet been proven, guys that were really out there, and some that seemed all right to me. What did I know anyway? I was just coming off a binge and needed some rest.

As soon as I got there, I got some cleaning supplies, scoured my cell and settled in for what I knew would be some time. I spent maybe a week in that place then I was put in a general population cell block. Thank you very much! Then it was more cleaning and getting as comfortable as possible in a concrete box.

All I did was play pinochle all day. It was seven weeks later that I was released into a twenty-eight-day alcohol program. There they found some marijuana paraphernalia and made accusations. This pompous witch who was the head of the program walked around in front of all forty of us with some sort of Judge Judy attitude telling us that if anyone didn't want to be there, she would be happy to tell their husband, wife, place of employment, or the court system that they'd completed the program and she'd fill out the necessary paperwork. She had accused me of the marijuana offense knowing I'd only been there about six days with no visitors. This really pissed me off and I let her know that it did. There were a few outside her office thinking about it when I walked up into her office. I was out of there within the hour and right back to the bottle.

Not very long after, I was at court to face those charges. A cop I knew told the judge "I know this man, and if he beat a guy like that, he must have deserved something." It went something like that, which is part of why I didn't get the eight years they'd been threatening me with. That's when I got three years' probation.

You don't know what this guy did, and although I knew this wouldn't come out too good for me, I couldn't stop what I did.

One Boring Sunday Night

The wrong place at the wrong time with the wrong face got me into a weird situation once when all I was doing was sitting at the bar. It was a typical Sunday night and I had just finished a lot of pool games with a man who called himself Tex.

He had a big cowboy hat and was a real gentleman. I beat him and he bought me a drink. I beat him again and I bought him one. A few more games and he left. That bar was one town away from mine but it was mostly patronized by our crowd. Disrupting the only sound in the place, which was the TV, the front door slammed open and in walked a very drunk guy from my town. I knew that guy but not real well. Right behind him was a cop from my town who was also very drunk and who held a gun on my homey. "Too bad," I thought "but better him than me!" The drunk cop directed John to sit on the bar stool next to me, so I thought it best to move. I started to stand up and he told me not to move or he would shoot me. I looked down and he had a .38 caliber revolver at waist level pointed at me. OK, been there done that! With that, I just turned around to wait for the police who he had just asked the bartender to call. Of course when they showed up, they were not his comrades because we were just over the line into the next town. Then they moved us outside to wait for his buddies to show up, and of course I knew them too. A detective from his police force came to his rescue. I knew that one since he'd been in uniform.

Outside with all the cops, they questioned me about my involvement in whatever break-in it may have been. Meanwhile, the detective was trying to cover up for his drunken coworker. He told me that guy was once his partner, blah, blah, blah. Yeah! So what I am a suspect and he had a gun on me.

Just then Tex came around the corner from the parking lot and I got him to verify my whereabouts for the last couple of hours. This Tex pulled out his A.B.C. identification and told them he had been in the bar undercover. I couldn't have had a better alibi.

Now this cop had a gun on me and I wasn't too happy about it. The detective wanted me to give his buddy a break so he could take him home. The other cops were standing off a bit waiting for my verdict on that guy. Now I was thinking how big the hole at the end of a gun barrel is when you're looking straight at it and I was still pretty upset with the guy. I knew this drunken cop needed this situation to go away, so I backed off. We all went home that night. I don't know whatever became of my homey with everything that happened. I guess he went home too.

Some months later I met the drunk cop in a hospital detox. I had gotten there a few days before and had good enough eyes to see that he really needed to be there. We didn't talk much about the incident but he remembered that it could have gone bad for him if I didn't let it go.

As much trouble as I was always getting into, I guess it was money in the bank!

Simple Insanity Turned Evil

So I was a thief? Of course I was! My alcohol consumption was so out of control that I couldn't go to work even if I was threatened with death. When I eventually woke up, if I wasn't still drunk, I was sick. Asked how I felt, I would just say, "Shoot me!" That is what I said for many mornings and meant it. I usually didn't have a job so I usually didn't have any money. I still needed a drink. So I would beg, borrow, and steal to get my booze. That was the only reason I would steal. I stole cars because I was stranded somewhere, and that was always my fault. Most of the time I could get a ride, but when I couldn't, I would always find a car.

One very cold night with snow and ice on the ground, I waited for someone to run into a store that had a line at the register. The one I picked must have had the exact change and came out right away to see me driving off in his car. I saw him coming and locked the door as he was about to open it. There was enough ice in the parking lot that I couldn't get traction. He hung on for some hundred yards, sliding on the ice himself. As soon as I hit the street, I'd have some traction and be gone. Just as I hit the pavement, I saw a black-and-white police car coming around the corner in time to see this guy hanging on to the door handle as I was dragging him down the street. Of course, I had to stop!

I made up a whopper of a story about how some guy asked me to move the car because he was blocked in. That really took quite a while! The guy even went to the police station, but all I got charged with was for taking the car without the owner's permission. I don't remember but I think they just let me out on what is called a R.O.R. (return on my own recognizance.) Here! Return this! I was a drunk and couldn't even make it to where I wanted to be, let alone somewhere I didn't want to be.

Of course I didn't show up on the court date and they issued a failure to appear warrant. They should have known better then to expect me to be there. I never showed up for a court date and they always issued the same warrant. Of course that only made it worse whenever they did get me because it was always an added fine to whatever the existing charge was at the time. There were never really any big fines except for the drunk driving on the revoked list. That usually made them very unhappy with me because I disobeyed their orders. Why this in particular I don't know because I disobeyed all their rules for the most part.

At age sixteen, I started stealing cars just for the thrill of it. There was this one car that we always took back to the train station so the guy would have a ride home after work, and then we'd go back and take it again. We took that car many times!

Then I finally got caught coming out of a blackout. I looked in the rearview mirror and seeing that a cop had lit me up, I panicked immediately. That was something I hardly ever did. I was so drunk and also very confused because I wasn't in the car I'd stolen earlier that same night (just another one I'd gotten away with).

After a high-speed chase, I busted though a roadblock and was on foot for about forty-five minutes. They caught me and were really unhappy with me to say the least. That was when I got maced from about two inches away while I had my hands cuffed behind my back in the backseat of the police car. That stinking punk bastard! That may be the only vulgarity you hear from me! Yeah! They were pissed, but that doesn't give them the right to become judge, jury, and executioner. That, they will always get away with!

You see it on all the cop shows. Some poor slob is standing there with his hands in the air and they will still slam him to the ground and throw a knee into the back of his neck and another to his lower back. Then, four, five, or six cops act like they are struggling to put the cuffs on him. When they are twisting his arms and fingers, they tell him to stop resisting. What a joke! I think a lot of them are sadists! Of course not all cops are bad and I should know. I've known some who are what cops should be, but I doubt there are many like that left. They all just follow their superiors. We all know about how one cop will never rat on another and they won't!

While "on tour" of the jails around the country, I've been treated fairly and unfairly. Some beatings weren't too bad but the worst was when I got maced. On the other hand, it was the same police force where I was treated most humanely. I was already locked down and had woken up from the floor when a cop came in to check on me (it was their routine because some guy had hanged himself in one of those cells.) It was about 3 a.m., when he asked me how I was feeling as I was getting up from the floor.

I remember saying, "None too good!"

To this he asked, "Do you think a drink would straighten you out?"

I told him, "Hell yeah!"

He just walked out. There were only six cells with three facing the other three. There was a guy in the one next to me, but I never saw him. There was a barred door, then a steel door. *Clink clank,* and the steel door opens, then the barred one. He opened my cell and motioned me out in the hallway to avoid the other inmate's eyes. Then he pulled a bottle of wine from his jacket and handed it to me. I chugged half of it and he grabbed it back. He obviously needed the rest for himself. What a guy! He knew what alcohol dependency was and had a heart! I went back to my cell with the wooden bed and slept till they came to take me to the county.

Par for the Course

just lived off my weekly pay; everything was uneventful until I stopped at a bar while taking some guys home on a Friday. Dry for about six months prior to that, I had about five or six shots in the half hour we were there. Early Saturday morning on my way back to work, I stopped at a bar for a few drinks I thought I needed. We were done early afternoon, so I stopped at a bar that was closer to home but still ten miles away. A few drinks there and all of a sudden, I realized how drunk I was. We lived in a motel and when I got there, I was so glad that I hadn't gotten another drunk driving arrest. I needed some sleep. My girl wasn't there but came in a minute later. All she said was "Where were you?" and scratched my face till it bled. It was after dark then. I was drunk, bleeding, and brainless. I didn't know what to do or how to react so I knocked her down and ran out the door. She kicked my car as I drove off.

I had planned on going to see my brother in prison some 200 miles away the next day, so I headed that way till I needed to stop. I got off the big road to a country road and pulled into a church parking lot. With the car turned off, there was only the black of night. I thought no one would bother me there, but I left the keys in the ignition to be safe. Big mistake! Right on the arrest report was that they had trouble waking me up to charge me with drunk driving. They left my car there and locked me up until I bailed out the next morning.

Two weeks later when I was scheduled to be in court, I was in jail in another state for another driving under the influence charge. That would not have happened but for a very crooked bunch of cops in the South (me and my Yankee address). I stayed there for forty-seven days, missing another court date.

That was one of the states with a big surcharge (robbery) on these charges. They also charged me again for the crime I already gave forty-seven days of my life to. I was a drunk and there was no way I could ever pay. I just had to ignore their request for all the money. It is now twenty-five years later and with interest, the charges are over $10,000.00.

This is a big headache and has been for a long time due to many prior offenses. In thirty years and in many states, I have earned seven first offenses out of eleven. The last was ten years ago; costly speeders is all I get now.

I still speed every time I drive. Sure I can learn, but I never pay attention.

Just as life gradually got worse, it gradually got better. I began to frequent a church and then moved out of state. Many years later, I began to attend another church more regularly until I joined.

I am still new at this and make no claim to having been enlightened. I do know that by the grace of God, I am no longer who I used to be I don't go where I went nor do what I did. My reactions are not the same.

I think it all began with a new gratitude I had for another recovery. As life got better again, I had even more gratitude for each new day. I became less selfish and more honest. I was more reliable and more charitable; I say please in the morning and thank you at night.

Today I just hope I can live long enough to outdo all the wrong I had done, and with God's continued grace, enjoy what's left of my life.

Rap Sheet

Suppose you picked up a guy's police record and started to read the list of charges. Reading between the lines are the not mentioned methods of arrests the time served before making bail, the cost in dollars and disgrace, etcetera. Those records cannot all be accurate because I've seen some of mine and there is some inaccuracy. There were wrong dates, sentences, and a few innocents that were recorded as guilty. Excuse me, but contrary to my faith, I have probably lied in court after swearing under oath. I believe most people lie under oath, allowing for the "just cause" and all.

There is much turmoil here! As time goes by, life may calm down a bit but there is always damage to the spirit of a man as these penalties are lived out.

You read further down the guy's rap sheet and here he is in trouble for the same thing again, same but ironically different this time. A beating, no bail, a longer jail time, more lost friends, and the next thing you read is that the guy is in jail in another state 1,000 miles away. You keep reading and there are more charges, more years, and more states. The average reader would naturally assume that the man mentioned in the paper is an idiot as much as he is a scourge.

Wait a minute! There has been a big change made here. Excuse me, but maybe it has been longer than a minute, more like twenty-five years, but still he is a work in progress. If you really could look at the big picture, you'd see the change in this man, whether you thought he deserved all the breaks in life that he got or not. For what this man did, no he did not deserve such good luck. Never did he realize how lucky he was. Luck, fate, God's plan, or whatever you see it as, it can't really be explained.

Turning to page 27 of that rap sheet and it gets a bit sparse. Another page and it is blank. There are a few "setbacks," but the years go by and there now are blank pages.

Now I imagine we all hope that there would be another list; sadly, one we never get to see. These are about all the good things the same guy has done since he stopped adding to that other list. Just use your imagination!

If you could personify these two lists, these two people would never be friends or be in the same circle of friends. I did get a new heart and a new mind. Who did it or what did it? Is this who or what responsible for the "bad seed" of the man before the change? If the change is entirely human, it could be physical because I never would have figured it out.

I just can't imagine how it's all done but I'm so glad for the blank pages.

"I am a new man."

Always a New Job

Go find a job. Yes, sure! I'll be right back. Where I come from, I could walk out of one job into the next one fast and easy. I had so many jobs that I couldn't even remember them all. After I got a felony conviction, I had to lie about where I had been in between some of the jobs I had listed. I got bored so easily. A new place of employment was fun until the newness wore off. In my early twenties, I already had changed jobs a lot; an interest in chemistry landed me in the control laboratory of two factories, some other menial work and then a second felony conviction. From then on the only thing that was true on a job application was my name. All the rest was made up while I was writing it. Only one time while working in a department store did I get fired after thirty days for falsifying. Dates, years, names, and places that were listed were all lies and that workplace was the only one that checked. In most places, I'd quit in a while anyway.

There were many jobs doing commercial or industrial roofing, driving trucks and cabs, iron worker, boat dock, auto salvage yard, auto parts counter sales, household goods, and freight tender. In some factories forklift driver, dental lab, assembly lines and different types of construction labor.

There was always a hustle of some kind but I did end up homeless a few times. I may have said it before; it was not boring but much of this stuff I could have done without.

At least I know I don't need to do it again. For now, I am a gardener.

Dear Readers,

After reading this book, I am sure you are stunned and possibly wondering how this author is still alive and well today. Needless to say, so are we.

I have known the author of this book for over fifty years. As you can see after reading this story, it has very little order to it. It mirrors the author's life, which had no order whatsoever to it. This is a *true* story of one man's journey from living with an abusive father to alcoholism which brought him to the pitfalls of his life. He fought alcoholism; it was a very long hard battle. At times it was one he didn't want to win He wanted to stay in that hellish romance with alcohol. It was all he had for comfort. Life may have gotten him down, and he may have been his own worst enemy, yet a greater power was watching over him to bring him to where he is today. He has come full circle back to the wonderful man he was as a youth, wiser yet the same.

Today he lives each day to its fullest in the capacity he's comfortable with. He serves in soup kitchens, belongs to a church, and follows his heart. His family is always in his mind's eye now unlike those many years when we lost him to alcohol. His friends are important to him now as they used to be before that disease ate at his mind, body, and soul. We are ecstatic to have him back with us again, he was dearly missed.

The penning of this book was done because of his inspiration to hopefully save even just *one*! Just *one* person from the pitfalls of hell, which he lived through because of his own doing He regrets each and every day of his life where he begged, borrowed, and stole from innocent people, even the not so innocent. Back then, it didn't matter. It was all about him. The people he met during his long years of alcoholism were never his friends. They were users as he was. Today he can hold his head high when he calls someone his friend, knowing they are true friends to him and he to them. These people stood by him, or knew him and have

111

taken him back under their wings and into their family units where he always belonged. They are the epitome of real friendship.

Today a new and bright light shines on him and he thinks of others first. He is "clean." This in itself should prove to many that anyone reading this book, knowing of an alcoholic or drug addict, or is one *can* turn their lives around. *He did!* Today his family and friends are proud of who he has become. He is once again the Mr. Personality we all love and whose friendship we cherish.

I will leave you with these words: "Do not go where the path may lead you, go instead where there is no path and leave a trail" (Ralph Waldo Emerson).

A Friend

About the Author

Sonny Carbo was born in Elizabeth, New Jersey. He is a retired part-time handyman.

As he struggled with bouts of depression, Sonny evaluated who he was, what he was, and realized what had to change. It was over the course of seventeen years that he hunkered down to begin his career as a writer.

With the inspiration of his mother, the kindness of one special lady from his church, and the support of a lifelong cousin-in-law, Sonny made the commitment to improve his life, and to begin writing.

In his spare time, he enjoys motorcycles and volunteering within his community.

Lightning Source UK Ltd.
Milton Keynes UK
UKHW04f0611160718
325764UK00001B/97/P